What th

"As I read your book I felt a weight lifting from me. My eyes were opened and I began to breathe more freely. The light became much brighter and God's will for me much clearer. Your book is the best penned explanation of true Christianity I have ever read. I can't thank you enough for your efforts to produce this inspired work."   Harold Wise   May 2014

"God has blessed me to know the author of a remarkable new book which asks and answers questions that I have wondered about in over half a century while teaching and establishing churches in four nations. The author is "speaking the truth in love" while "avoiding foolish questions that gender strife." Brother Ensor has effectively handled the "unwritten traditions" that bind us, setting us free to examine again in a fresh light the everlasting Gospel."   Don Wright, Missionary Evangelist   April 2014

"From cover-to-cover, **Taking Another Look** prompts chuckles, tears and laughter. Metaphorically, Dennis has run for a hundred yard touchdown. He provides here a fresh yet nuanced treatment of the age-old discussion about Christianity. Readers will be challenged to detach from opinions and approach scripture with boldness. This is exceptional!"
Raymon D. Fullerton III   Community Enrichment Minister, New York City, April 2014

"I thought my son wasn't interested in religion as every time I tried to talk to him he got mad at me. After discussing your book with him today I found out he is very religious minded but is opposed to the strict rules binding our beliefs. The church he grew up in was just bound up in rules and regulations. Your book has opened up in him a whole new perspective on religious beliefs. We talked very freely for the first time about religion."
N.K.   April 2014

TAKING ANOTHER LOOK AT NEW TESTAMENT CHRISTIANITY

TAKING ANOTHER LOOK AT NEW TESTAMENT CHRISTIANITY

Dennis Ensor

Hamilton, Texas

Dennis Ensor publishing, Hamilton, TX 76531

© 2014 Dennis Ensor. All rights reserved. No part of this book may be reproduced or transmitted in any form or by any means, electronic or mechanical, including photocopying, recording or by any information storage and retrieval system, without written permission from the author, except for the inclusion of brief quotations in a review.

Published 2014
Printed in the United States of America

Cover and interior design, Dennis Ensor
Contact email: tal@dennisensor.com
Website: www.tal.dennisensor.com

Printed in the United States of America
ISBN- paperback - 9781499157024
First Edition

Dedication

*This book is dedicated to my dad, **James Ellis Ensor**, who went on to be with the Lord thirty-two years ago today, April 30, 1982. He was a man of God who instilled in me and my siblings the desire to be like him—to love others, to make a positive difference in people's lives, and to bring glory to God.*

Acknowledgments

It would be impossible for me to list all the wonderful friends and loved ones (and "adversaries") who have helped shaped my thinking through the years. Most of you know who you are and know the roles you have played. Thank you for being the iron that helped sharpen my thinking.

To those of you who spent countless hours reading this book multiple times, making corrections and suggestions in pursuit of perfection, thank you from the bottom of my heart. These include Billie Ensor, Raymon Fullerton, Tim Tutor, ND Kelso and Bobby Lee. You are awesome!

To whatever degree readers are positively impacted by this endeavor, just know that you have contributed to that. You have made a difference, directly or indirectly, through this work. I pray God's blessings on you as you continue making a difference 'til Jesus comes. Amen!

Table of Contents

Preface—Our Heritage	**13**
Introduction	**19**
Little Red Flags	**24**
First Day of the Week	25
Desiring to be an Elder	28
Authorized Name of the Church	29
No Creeds but the Bible	37
Who is my Brother?	**44**
Innies	45
Outies	49
Deniers of the Heart of the Gospel	51
Blatantly Immoral People	53
Divisive Spirits and Binders of Belief	55
Refusers of Correction	57
Contending for the Faith	**59**
False Teachers and Doctrines	63
Fruit Inspectors	69
The Weak Brother	73
Worldly—Infants in Christ	75

Gold or Straw	77
How to Treat Those Who Disagree	79
Keep in Fellowship When	81
Understanding God's Will	**83**
Multiple Interpretation Methods	85
God Means What He Says	87
Greet One Another With a Holy Kiss	95
Customs and Culture Versus Command	101
Examples	107
Necessary Inference	113
Speak Where the Bible Speaks	117
A Better Way	121
Regulations for Worship	**129**
Old Testament Regulations for Worship	131
New Testament Regulations for Worship	137
Rule Keeping Worship	145
K.I.S.S.	149
The 80/20 Rule	157
A Message to Adult Bible Class Teachers	**159**
Post Script	**163**

Preface

Until about twenty years ago, I had been under the strong impression that in the early eighteen hundreds two men, Barton W. Stone and Alexander Campbell, had done an amazing thing. These two men, each with a large following, independently of each other, had decided to go back to the Bible and start fresh in their efforts to understand exactly what it taught.

The outcomes of their independent studies, as I understood it, led them to agree almost unanimously on every point. When their paths crossed and they compared notes, they joyfully decided to join forces to the glory of God. From that point on, they and all their followers restored New Testament Christianity to what it was in the first century.

As a result (again, as I understood it) was that we, in the Church of Christ today, are part of that restored New Testament Christianity, and the things we believe to be sound doctrine today are the exact things that Stone and Campbell had agreed were sound doctrine back then. The church has been in its restored state for the past two hundred years, virtually unchanged.

It makes a good story. It is powerful when told from the pulpit like that. When I heard it way back then I felt good about being part of that one true church, and about preaching sound doctrine. But the story is not exactly true. It is the Hollywood version of what really happened.

What helped me understand the real version of what happened was a great little book by C. Leonard Allen called, *Distant Voices: Discovering a Forgotten Past for a Changing Church*.[1]

Allen went back into historical documents and letters and discovered some writings of Stone, Campbell and others which revealed a much more complex chain of events and a much more diverse set of doctrinal beliefs than I had been lead to believe.

Though it is true that they did unite as brothers in Christ, there are striking differences in their doctrinal beliefs, differences which often led to sharp tensions between them, both in the years before and after the union. And yet, even with these differences, they held each other in high esteem as brothers in Christ.

Stone, in particular, would not be welcomed as a member in many of our modern day Churches of Christ, especially the more conservative ones. Many positions he held on various doctrines would be considered very "liberal," to say the least. I have no doubt that in today's world many would receive warnings about the "false teachings" of this "dangerous" man.

Even Campbell held some views which would go against the grain of many conservative churches today. For example, neither he nor Stone were necessarily willing to exclude from eternal salvation unimmersed believers. This position would raise some eyebrows today, and would have done so even more in the mindset of 20th century Churches of Christ.

Stone and Campbell believed that there was room for a wide diversity of opinion in the church, or they would not have joined together as brothers. They agreed, and demonstrated, that even the most sincere and diligent students of the Word might not agree at many points.

I also have come to that conclusion. I have seen too many wonderful men of God, men who were diligent in their study but who came to different conclusions on various topics. Of course, the problem is not in the Word, but in the interpreters of the Word, men. We will talk more about that later.

By the 1850s, many preachers had come to believe that the conclusions of Bible study could be, and should be, exact, and that there was no room for debate. I have come across a few people who have the same mindset. They believe they have got it down and there is not even a need to reconsider their doctrinal positions.

When I asked one fellow, "What if we both study very diligently on a scripture with open minds and open hearts and come to different conclusions?" He said, "Then you will need to study a little more." Unfortunately, he was not joking.

The problem created by this mindset came about because not all these preachers could agree on what the undeniably-correct conclusions should be. Rather than conclude that it was possible that godly men could agreeably disagree, hard lines were drawn. Churches split. Division reigned.

Unfortunately, this rigid mindset is still prevalent among the more conservative members in Churches of Christ. That is why there are two or three Churches of Christ in every small town in the Bible belt.

Stone and Campbell held that there should be unity in faith, but liberty in opinions. I think they were right. But there should also be a continued effort to come to a common understanding of what God really wants. And that is what **Taking Another Look at New Testament Christianity** is all about.

I admire Stone and Campbell for three things:

1. They never stopped searching for the truth. They were continually re-evaluating their doctrinal positions in light of new experiences and new understandings. They were willing to consider new ideas in their search for soundness.

2. They continued to respect each other and hold each other in high esteem, even when they disagreed on Bible doctrine.

3. They were open to the possibility of being wrong in their understanding of God's Word. When they realized they had been mistaken, they changed course.

If you are like Stone and Campbell in these three areas, still seeking, still respecting and still willing to change your course, this book is for you.

It is necessary for us to approach the Bible to learn what to believe rather than going there for confirmation of what we already believe.
—Harold Hazelip

Introduction

In May of 2012, ***The Good News From God: A Fresh Perspective on the Bible, Christianity, Church and Life***, was published. Though I, the author of what you are now reading, would be considered the primary author of that *Good News* book, it was a collaborative effort among the Outreach church of Christ members, as well as a few friends and family.

The book was designed for two groups of readers—those who are looking for answers to basic questions about the Bible, Christianity, church and the abundant life, and those who already have those answers, but are looking for, perhaps, a better way to share that knowledge with others.

The first group is made up of people who are ready to learn: some who now have small children at home and feel a need for direction, and a change in lifestyle, to properly raise those children; some who have experienced one or more life-changing events, such as a divorce, the loss of a job, radical health issues or the death of a loved one. These difficult challenges have awakened them to the need to find God. For whatever reason, they are ready to make a change and are seeking guidance.

The second group is comprised of good-hearted believers who want to share the gospel, but are uncomfortable doing so. It may be that, though they understand the Bible well enough for themselves, they feel inadequate in their ability to teach others.

They may be hesitant to intrude into someone's life for fear that they may offend. They do not want to be pests and create a rift in personal or professional relationships, but desire to share God's good message.

The book was created to fill a need by putting all the key information into one easy-to-read, easy-to-understand and easy-to-share format.

With the Good News book, the person seeking a better way would not only find clear, concise answers to his questions about how it all fits together, but would receive guidance on the best way to move forward after receiving that basic information.

After the book was completed, Outreach church of Christ, with an average weekly attendance of sixty-two, decided to distribute the Good News book as an outreach ministry. We committed to making the book available, free of charge, to all, as long as funds were available.

The response has been nothing short of amazing. In the less than two years since the first order of ten copies was delivered (on May 23, 2012) approximately ninety thousand Good News books have been distributed (in eight languages: English, Spanish, Chinese, Arabic, French, Italian, German, Telugu [India], with more in the works). And the demand continues to grow. **Praise God!**

Though acceptance of the Good News book in Churches of Christ has been wide-spread, that acceptance has not been unanimous. There is a handful of Christians who have generally felt uncomfortable with a couple of things—one, a statement about the Holy Spirit (whom everyone receives upon baptism).

The statement causing discomfort is, "If you are in a church and it just does not feel right, it may be that the Spirit is telling you that this is not the right place." This is not definitive, but merely a "maybe the Spirit is telling you" statement. Not everyone has been in agreement with even a remote possibility of a Holy Spirit-directed "feel right" moment.

I do not know if the Spirit puts a "feel right" sign in our hearts. But it seems reasonable that he may. We do have a case in Acts 16:13-15, where Paul began to speak with some women who had gathered at the river. Lydia was one of the women there, and *The Lord opened her heart to respond to Paul's message.*

It is unknown to me how this was manifested. But it seems very reasonable that Lydia would have had a very strong, Spirit-led, feeling that she should listen and respond to Paul's message. If it was not through a Spirit-led feeling, how else could the Lord open her heart to respond to Paul's message? It was the Lord who opened her heart. How could it have been anything but a Spirit-implanted feeling?

A second element prompting discomfort originated from what a few readers felt was missing, not from what was written. The book, according to the some, does not go far enough in getting the baptized believers into the Church of Christ.

The thought is that, unless the book gives more guidance to the new Christian, these new believers could just as easily wind up in a "denomination" as they could the Church of Christ. The fear is that we would have brought them this far along and then left them short of the goal. Why take the chance? Why not bring them all the way home? And that is their concern.

Having grown up in the Church of Christ, I was expecting blow-back on these two fronts—possibly a lot—though only a little has come. It is just that, through the years I have come to the conclusion that, in its purest sense, the traditional Church of Christ doctrine in that regard has not been completely accurate. I do not think the Bible is in alignment with that doctrine, *per se*.

There are other areas in which I have become uncomfortable with traditional Church of Christ conclusions. Rather than ignoring those areas while dealing with these, I decided that now is the time for me to sit down and pull my thoughts together for the purpose of engaging you in a discussion about how we have been doing things and how it is time to step back and take a second look at some of those things.

For the good of all, we need to talk. Perhaps you can show me the errors in my thinking. I am open to that. I am not trying to have it my way. I am trying to understand God's will.

If your thoughts cause me to realign, I will be thankful. I have nothing to lose. I just want to know the truth. I hope you feel the same way, if it goes the other way. Maybe God put me here "for just such a time as this" (Esther 4:14)—to open your eyes to a better way of looking at these things.

Either way, it is time for us to do what those noble Bereans did, to test everything and hold on to the good. I want to make it clear that I do not have a great feud going on with the Church of Christ. I do not have a deep-seated frustration or hatred of or animosity toward the Church of Christ.

There is nothing like that in my bones. But I do think that there are a few areas in which we have missed the boat—that we have implied, or stated, that the scriptures mean something when, in fact, they do not mean that at all.

So, it is my hope that you join me in reconsidering these things. I promise to be respectful. I am just looking for the truth, for common sense-reality in light of God's Word. And I promise to be as straightforward as I can.

May God bless us as we seek his will for our lives.

Little Red Flags

Through the years I have heard a few statements from individuals who have taught me what certain things mean in the Bible. If I look at those things very precisely, which seems to be my nature, I cannot say those things really mean exactly what I was told they mean. Let me list a few.

1. First day of the week.

Acts 20:7 (NIV) *On the first day of the week we came together to break bread. Paul spoke to the people and, because he intended to leave the next day, kept on talking until midnight.*

All my life, I have been told that the New Testament says we should meet for worship on the first day of the week. Acts 20:7 is the scripture you always find in the margins after such a statement. I have a couple of things to say about that.

First of all, I have no problem with the fact that they met on the first day of the week, even of every week. Second, I have no problem with the fact that we still meet on the first day of the week, every week. It is a good thing to do.

But I do have a problem with any statement that says God commanded Christians to meet together on the first day of every week to worship, or to break bread. That is not a commandment I can find anywhere in the Word. To some, this may seem nit-picky, but it is not. It is reality. It is a fact.

When I look at Acts 20:7, it does not tell us to come together on the first day of the week. It tells us that *they* came together on the first day of the week. The context seems to indicate that this statement refers to this one particular incident when Paul came by, and it is not a command that we should do the same. I did see one translation that could be read in a way that indicated that they met on the first day of every week, but even that translation stopped short of making it a commandment for us to do so.

I am well aware of the passage in which the people were told to set aside a sum of money in keeping with his income on the first day of every week (1 Cor 16:2). I suppose you could meet this commandment at home. And I am well aware of the historical evidence that the first century church met together on the first day of every week.

I have no problem with us setting our meeting times on the first day of every week. But that is not the same thing as saying that we are commanded to meet together on the first day of every week to worship God; It is not the same as saying that everyone who does not meet together on the first day of every week is lost.

Surely you can agree with my point here. They met on the first day, but it was not a command to meet. Which leads to a question: Why was not God more command-oriented in this particular area?

How is it that this incredible God of detail would leave out something as simple and specific as, "I command you to assemble together on the first day of every week to worship the Lord?" Why would he leave that out?

I *may* speculate about why he left it out, but there is no doubt that he did leave it out. Later in the book we will be covering some new territory that might cause us to look back and say, "Oh, so that is why he left that commandment out." Until then, suffice it to say that if he left it out, who are we to put it in?

Let us keep meeting just like we have been, but not try to say it is a commandment to meet on the first day of every week or that you are lost if you do not.

2. An Elder should desire the office to be qualified for the office.

1 Tim. 3:1 (NIV) *Here is a trustworthy saying: If anyone sets his heart on being an overseer, he desires a noble task.*

The King James puts it as follows:

This is a true saying, If a man desire the office of a bishop, he desireth a good work.

This is another case in which I have heard it stated that one of the qualifications of an elder is that he must desire to be an elder. But I do not think that is what the passage is saying. The passage is saying that being an elder is a noble task. If one desires it, the thing he is desiring is noble.

Though I am an elder, a shepherd, I did not really desire to be one. But, when asked by the members of my home congregation to be one, I was willing to do it.

I try to do a good job at it, though I do not consider myself to be a leader. I am just an individual who is trying to be a Christian, trying to live a Godly life, and willing to be an elder as long as the congregation wants me to fill that role.

3. To be the one true church, you must have an authorized name.

Almost every book I have read about what is required to be part of the New Testament church talks about having an authorized name. Other books do not say that specifically, but the implication seems to be there, and the advocates of that point of view seem to feel very strongly about it. The primary verse quoted is **Roman 16:16 (NIV)**,

Salute one another with an holy kiss. The churches of Christ salute you.

The website

http://church-of-christ.org/church-of-christ/JMB.html
lists the following names that the church is called:

- The temple of God (1 Cor. 3:16)
- The bride of Christ (Ephesians 5:22-32)
- The body of Christ (Col. 1:18,24; Eph 1:22-23)
- The kingdom of God's son (Col. 1:13)
- The house of God (1 Tim. 3:15)
- The church of God (1 Cor. 1:2)
- The church of the first-born (Heb. 12:23)
- The church of the Lord (Acts 20:28)
- The churches of Christ (Rom. 16:16)

"Some Things You Should Know" is from a tract by Gospel Minutes, P.O. Box 50007, Ft. Worth, TX 76105-0007.

This statement that the church is called these "names" is a very accurate statement, in that those were the words used to describe the church of the first century. It is spot on, though the most common description is simply, "the church."

As an aside, there is another name listed in the New Testament that never seems to make the "names" list. There are five references to "the Way" in the book of Acts. For example, **Acts 19:23 (NIV)** *About that time there arose a great disturbance about the Way.* The other occurrences are in Acts 9:2; 19:9; 24:14; 24:22.

The references to "the Way" actually sound like they were used as a name more than any of the other names on the list, and yet it is usually ignored. I wonder why anyone would leave it off the list. It makes me scratch my head.

I have a few questions about how we, in the Church of Christ, have addressed the subject of having an authorized name for the church. I will touch on them here.

~~~~~

A. The common New Testament description of the church was simply "the church." If we would leave it at that, there would be no problem. What seems to go beyond scripture is a statement that often follows: "To be the one true church, you must have a name authorized by the scriptures."

In the paragraph below I have quoted a statement that was recommended as an addition to the *Good News* book.

If Christ is establishing His church, should it not have His name on it? And because Christ can be identified by several names in scripture, there are any number of names by which His church could be called. For ease in recognition, the title, church of Christ has been used for centuries.

In reality, this is an admission that there is no biblical requirement for the true church to have an authorized name as revealed in the New Testament. And yet, it is been my experience that, even though it is not required, the name of a religious group is the first thing we have used to either reject or accept a body of believers, a church of Christ.

The truth is, it is nothing more than a person's opinion that the church must have one of the names on the list to be acceptable to God—to be part of the one true church.

I do not believe I have the right to say one must attend a church that has a name from that list or he would not be a part of the one true church. For that reason there is no statement like that in *The Good News From God* book. It is just not in the Word, regardless of how badly we might wish it were. It is just not there.

~~~~~

B. If a church-name was important to God, why did he not list one name for his one church? Why would he give us a list of ten names for his one church? Could it be that he was trying to de-emphasize a specific naming of the church? Maybe he did not want a name at all, just a description. So why do we feel the need to legalize a name?

We have a tendency to turn named entities into institutions. We seem to convert active, vibrant organisms into rigid, stodgy institutions. The vibrancy leaves. The structure remains. I do not know if that is the answer, but still, God did not put an official name on his church. Why should we?

~~~~~

C. Is the Church of Christ the same as the (little "c") church of Christ? Are those two synonymous? When you see one, are you seeing the other? Is everyone who is a member of the Church of Christ a member of the church that Jesus established? Is the Church of God (or any of the other names on the list) the same as the church of Christ?

One thing is for sure: when you become a child of God, the Lord adds you to his church, his one and only church. This is true no matter where you are in the world. You could be in remotest Africa or in downtown Dallas. The Lord adds you to the church, his body, when you become his child.

Is that nullified if the building in which you worship with other baptized believers has a name on it that is not found among the names on the list? Think about it. The Lord adds you to the church.

When you become a child of God, he adds you to the church, period. And if he adds you to the church, you are part of his body, period.

~~~~~

D. The Lord established one church. But, obviously, there were many churches in the New Testament world. There were churches in Rome, in Corinth, in Galatia and in many other places. There were some who met in people's homes. They were all over the place—these *many* churches.

So, a question: Is the fact that there were multiple churches in the first century on par with the fact that there are multiple churches in the twenty-first century?

All the churches in the first century were part of the one true church. At least, I do not know of any situation where there were other churches outside of the "one church" at the time.

Also, there are many churches in the twenty-first century

that are part of the "one church" that the Lord established in the first century. The difference is that, in the twenty-first century, there are likely to be some churches that are truly not part of that "one church." If that is the case, the challenge is to sort out which of those churches are part and which are not part of that one church. Right?

Traditionally, the first way we have sorted out the "true churches" from the "false churches" was by the name on the building. It is my hope that, because we now clearly see that this is not a biblically sanctioned practice, we have decided to discontinue using this method to determine which church is true.

This leads us to the second way we have evaluated churches to determine their authenticity.

4. No Creeds But the Bible

The second way in which we have sorted churches is by how they've conducted their worship services. If they get that one hour a week right, we have considered them as part of the one true church. If not, then not.

Though we have always said we have no creed but the Bible, the truth is that we have had an unwritten creed and that the true churches must have a creed very similar to ours or we will reject them. Let me show you what I mean:

All of the books I have read about the Church of Christ had a chapter with the title "No Creeds But the Bible." The fact that we have never had a written creed, a practice different from that of most other religious groups, was deemed to be one of the proofs that we are, indeed, the "true church" of the New Testament. We are a church that just went by the God-inspired Bible, not by a man-inspired document or code.

Over the years, it began to dawn on me that, even though we have never had a *written* creed, we have most definitely had an *unwritten* one. It was one that, even though it theoretically did not exist, everybody knew when somebody violated it. Without exception, there would be consequences when those lines were crossed.

Since I had grown up with the unwritten code, the enforcement of it seemed perfectly reasonable and justifiable from a practical standpoint, because we never even noticed it existed. It just was. But when I noticed that it existed, and began writing it down, it seemed a little comical in some ways.

In fact, when written down, it seemed to come alive as a set of rules by men without direct scriptural basis. Let me illustrate what I mean.

According to our heritage, our Christian lives are broken down into two basic categories. They are as follows:

(**Note**: These things are not what I necessarily believe are correct as far as Bible teaching is concerned, but I believe that they accurately describe our religious thought patterns. I just want to describe what I perceive to be our traditional views.)

Two Basic Categories of Christian Living

1. Worship Services ("five acts of worship")
    A. Singing
    B. Praying
    C. Preaching
    D. Lord's Supper
    E. Giving

2. Daily Lives

    A. The Do List:— Visit the sick and in prison, help the poor, etc.

    B. The Do Not List:—-Steal, Cheat, Lie, Commit Adultery, Hate, etc. (aka "We don't smoke, we don't chew, and we don't go with the girls that do.")

These categories are not unique to the Church of Christ, but are believed and practiced by many religious groups today. What sets the "Church of Christ" apart from the others is the specific requirements involved in three of the "five acts of worship," plus the method required to become part of the church. I call these four items the "Church of Christ Corner Posts." I will list them beginning on the next page.

Church of Christ Corner Posts
(Items absolutely necessary for our salvation.)

    1. **Baptism** (immersion only, for remission of sins)

    2. **Singing** (without instrumental music. In some places also without clapping, swaying, raising hands, etc.)

    3. **Lord's Supper** (taken every Sunday. Some places restrict the fruit of the vine to one cup, or sometimes two)

    4. **Male Leadership** (in all aspects of the worship services)

Few in the "Church of Christ" would argue with any of these descriptions (although there has been a gradual shift on 2 and 4).

In addition to these primary "corner posts," we have some "pillars" that are important but do not carry as much weight as do the corner posts. Most, but not necessarily all congregations practice these:

Church of Christ Pillars

1. The main worship service is Sunday morning for about one hour. Only baptized males can lead or serve the congregation in one of the five acts of worship during this worship service. It used to be that these baptized males had to wear a coat and tie to be acceptable but that requirement has faded away in most congregations.

> A very wise friend, George T., once told me of a time when he, as an elder, was approached by a sister about how we should require everyone who serves communion to wear a coat and tie. George asked, "But what if they do not own a coat and tie?" She said, "We could have a few extras hanging in the preparation room for them to borrow." George said, "Maybe we could just have a set of robes for everyone to use." The sister turned and walked away and never brought it up again. (For those of you who are less familiar with the Church of Christ, we would not be caught dead in a religious robe. For some reason, those are not allowed in the "one true church.")

2. There is generally a Bible study class before (or sometimes after) the worship service. It is not a worship service, but Bible Study is required during this time. Alternate activities are not permitted except on rare occasions.

(In some Churches of Christ, no Bible class is allowed since there is no record of Bible classes in the New Testament, but these churches are the exception rather than the rule.)

3. Another worship service is held on Sunday evening. It is not as important as the one on Sunday morning (evidently) because less people come and even young non-baptized males can, for training purposes, participate in each activity (except serving communion for those who missed the main service that morning).

4. Another worship service/Bible study class is held on Wednesday evening. It is also, evidently, not as important as the Sunday morning worship service.

5. No crosses or religious symbols shall be placed in the building.

6. Little or no social activities are permitted during the times designated for "worship services," or during class time (which is not considered a "worship service.")

7. The worship service must be officially closed, usually with a closing prayer, before any special events such as a choral singing, drama event, husband and wife marriage presentation, children reciting memory work in front of congregation, etc., can take place.

8. Announcements are okay during any of the worship services.

These additional pillars are not considered quite as critical as the first four corner posts but they, none the less, should be observed.

That sums up our unwritten creed. If a church does not abide by these creedal rules, it is obviously not part of the true church that Jesus established in the first century. At least, that has been the application in my experience.

It now becomes apparent that, in spite of our claim to the contrary, we have truly had our own unwritten creed, a creed primarily focused on a set of man-made "rules for worship" during a very small period of time on the first day of each week.

Any church that does not follow these practices is considered outside the boundaries of the one, "true church," especially if that church does not have a name listed in the Bible—in reality, the "Church of Christ."

(We have apparently felt, or at least our body language has signaled, that if we get that one hour of the week right, everything else will take care of itself. If we get that one hour wrong, we are not part of the one true church. It is time to rethink that model. It is time to get back into the Word to see if there might not be a better way.)

So how do we know if a church is part of the New Testament church? Let us think about that. Since it is Jesus who adds every member to his church, and since every member is part of the body of Christ, the church, would it not follow that the church is everywhere any member is? Maybe not. I need to think about that some more.

As a follow-up: I have noticed that many of us automatically determine that anyone who belongs to a "denomination" (is lost, that he is not my brother in Christ, because he goes to a "denomination." (A "denomination" is considered as a religious body devised and organized by man, not God.) We reject him for other reasons too, creed-related things. I will have more to say about those things later.

In the next chapter I would like for us to re-examine just who is my brother, and at what point does he stop being my brother—according to the Word.

Who Is My Brother?*

*Please Note: In this book I will use the term "brother" in a generic sense—as in "brother(s) and/or sister(s)"—except in a very few specific and obvious cases. I do this for the sake of simplicity and textual flow. I mean no offense to my awesome sisters in Christ.

"Innies"

It has been my experience that people in the Church of Christ have been exclusive regarding whom they include as fellow Christians. That is loosening up some (though some would say with a sadness that, "It is being watered down, diluted.")

It has been a while since I heard anyone say the words "We are the only ones going to heaven." I am sure there are many who still believe that, but I have not been in such environments where that mind-set is as prevalent as it used to be.

My purpose for doing this particular study is not so much to determine who is my brother as it is to determine who is **not** my brother according to scriptures. I want to look at what point someone stops being my brother—according to scripture (as opposed to Church of Christ tradition). At what point do we "get to" exclude someone?

Before I can get to that, we need to establish who *is* my brother. We are looking for "Innies" and "Outies" here. So the first question is "How does one become a child of God, and my brother?" How does one get to be an "Innie?" I have included some pertinent parts of key verses. I do not think most of us will have a problem with any of these items.

Mk. 16:15-16 (NIV) *He said to them, Go into all the world and preach the good news to all creation. Whoever **believes and is baptized** will be saved, but whoever does not believe will be condemned.*

Acts 2:36-37,38,41 (NIV) *Therefore let all Israel be assured of this: God has made this Jesus, whom you crucified, both Lord and Christ. When the people heard this, they were cut to the heart and said to Peter and the other apostles, "Brothers, what shall we do?" Peter replied, **"Repent and be baptized**, every one of you, in the name of Jesus Christ for the forgiveness of your sins. And you will receive the gift of the Holy Spirit".. . . Those who accepted his message were baptized, and about three thousand were added to their number that day.*

Rom. 10:9-10 (NIV) *That if you **confess with your mouth, "Jesus is Lord," and believe in your heart that God raised him from the dead**, you will be saved. For it is with your heart that you believe and are justified, and it is with your mouth that you confess and are saved.*

Gal 3:26-27 (NIV) *You are all sons of God through faith in Christ Jesus, for all of you who were **baptized** into Christ have clothed yourselves with Christ.*

Who is my brother? Anyone who believes that Jesus is the Christ, the son of God, has confessed that Jesus is Lord, repented of his sins, and has been baptized is a Christian, a child of God and, therefore, my brother in Christ.

Rom. 8:1-2 (NIV) *Therefore, there is now **no condemnation** for those who are in Christ Jesus, because through Christ Jesus the law of the Spirit of life set me free from the law of sin and death.*

According to this scripture, if anyone is in Christ Jesus, there is no condemnation for him. None. Zero. Nada.

And, as stated in **Acts 2:47 (NKJV)**, when someone has done these things, it is the Lord who has added him to the church.

Acts 2:47 (NKJV) *. . . praising God and having favor with all the people. And the Lord added to the church daily those who were being saved.*

And the church is not the building. It is his people. We, the Christians, are the church and the body of Christ.

1 Cor. 12:27 (NIV) *Now you are the body of Christ, and each one of you is a part of it.*

When I am seeking the lost, this is exactly what I teach, because this is what the Bible clearly teaches—and I cannot imagine ever seeing it differently. To be a Christian, one must hear the gospel, repent of his sins, confess that Jesus is the Christ, the son of God and be buried with him in baptism at which time he receives the gift of the Holy Spirit and the Lord adds him to his one true church. Period.

Note: *If someone tells me he is a Christian, I accept him as my Brother without quizzing him about these matters. Even if he has not understood the scriptures completely on this matter (because of what the person who taught him had said). I believe it is God who ultimately decides who is my brother.*

I feel a responsibility to always teach what I have stated above (prior to this side note). If someone is in error about being my brother, I believe that I stand a much better chance to teach him the way more correctly if we are on "brotherly" terms. After all, the objective is to get to heaven and to take as many others with me as I can. If he will not listen to what I have to say because I have rejected him first, then I have blown my chance to make a positive difference.

I am not asking you to agree or disagree on my approach here. I am just doing the best I can to be what God wants me to be.

"Outies"

When does someone cease to be my brother?

Next, I would like to examine what should be the criteria, according to the Bible, regarding the point at which we cannot, or should no longer, accept someone as a brother. Is it if he uses instrumental music? Is it if he worships with a "denominational" group outside of the Church of Christ? Is it if he believes in speaking in tongues? What, according to the scriptures, removes him from being a Christian and from being my brother?

In my growing up years (and for many years since) we, in the Church of Christ, were fairly exclusive about whom we would consider to be our fellow Christians. I have heard the phrase, "It is a shame that they are not Christians" used about people who believed just like I do and had been baptized, except that they had a piano in their church building and they had a different name on the door. Is that the Biblical criteria for not being a brother?

Let us consider the question, "What about those who have taken all the necessary steps to become a Christian, but believe differently than we do on doctrinal issues?" At what point does one "fall out" of the church? At what point do I draw the line in determining those with whom I can fellowship and worship? What are the essential elements we *must* have in common? Let us look at the scriptures to see where the lines were drawn.

According to the Bible, we are to include as part of our brotherhood those who have followed the teaching in **1 Cor. 15:1-8 (NIV).**

Now, brothers, I want to remind you of the gospel I preached to you, which you received and on which you have taken your stand. By this gospel you are saved, if you hold firmly to the Word I preached to you. Otherwise, you have believed in vain. For what I received I passed on to you as of first importance: that Christ died for our sins according to the Scriptures, that he was buried, that he was raised on the third day according to the Scriptures, and that he appeared to Peter, and then to the Twelve. After that, he appeared to more than five hundred of the brothers at the same time, most of whom are still living, though some have fallen asleep. Then he appeared to James, then to all the apostles, and last of all he appeared to me also, as to one abnormally born.

This passage is the beginning of a response by Paul to a group evidently teaching that there will be no resurrection. Paul makes a very logical argument against this belief in the rest of Chapter 15 (vs12-19, ff). What is key about this passage (15:1-8) is that it reveals necessary beliefs which one must have to be saved. Paul stresses these beliefs by reminding them that he passed these beliefs on to them as of **"first importance."** These are not optional items. This is the heart of the gospel.

We have some specific examples in the New Testament of people who would fall into that excluded category because of their denial of the heart of the gospel. They are as follows:

1. Exclude people whose belief denies the heart of the gospel.

    A. 2 Jn. 1:7-11 (NIV) *Many deceivers, who do not acknowledge Jesus Christ as coming in the flesh, have gone out into the world. Any such person is the deceiver and the antichrist. Watch out that you do not lose what you have worked for, but that you may be rewarded fully. Anyone who runs ahead and does not continue in the teaching of Christ does not have God; whoever continues in the teaching has both the Father and the Son. If anyone comes to you and does not bring this teaching, do not take him into your house or welcome him. Anyone who welcomes him shares in his wicked work.*

    B. 2 Tim. 2:16-18 (NIV) Hymanaeus and Philetus were Christians who were teaching that the resurrection was already past.

Avoid godless chatter, because those who indulge in it will become more and more ungodly. Their teaching will spread like gangrene. Among them are Hymenaeus and Philetus, who have wandered away from the truth. They say that the resurrection has already taken place, and they destroy the faith of some.

    C. 1 Tim. 1:19-20 (NIV) Hymanaeus and Alexander were Christians who had rejected their faith and good conscience, and had blasphemed.

. . . holding on to faith and a good conscience. Some have rejected these and so have shipwrecked their faith. Among them are Hymenaeus and Alexander, whom I have handed over to Satan to be taught not to blaspheme.

D. Jude 1:4 (NIV) speaks of Godless men who change grace into license for immorality and deny Jesus Christ:

For certain men whose condemnation was written about long ago have secretly slipped in among you. They are godless men, who change the grace of our God into a license for immorality an deny Jesus Christ our only Sovereign and Lord.

E. 1 Jn. 2:18-26 (speaks of men who are liars, the antichrist, who are trying to lead Christians away)

Who is the liar? It is the man who denies that Jesus is the Christ.

One cannot deny the heart of the gospel (as stated in 1 Cor. 15:1-8) and **still** be my brother.

2. Exclude people who live blatantly immoral lives.

We are also authorized to reject people if they live blatantly and obviously ungodly lives. We need to be careful that we disfellowship people only because of what is stated explicitly in the scriptures, **not** because of opinions about things that are not so explicitly stated.

A. 1 Cor. 5:1-5,13 a man who was a church member was **living with his father's wife**. Paul clearly rejects this, something which we can not tolerate in our membership. The man who does this must be rejected.

B. Gal. 5:19-21 (NIV) tells us *The acts of the sinful nature are **obvious:** sexual immorality, impurity and debauchery; idolatry and witchcraft; hatred, discord, jealousy, fits of rage, selfish ambition, dissensions, factions and envy; drunkenness, orgies, and the like. I warn you, as I did before, that those who live like this will not inherit the kingdom of God.*

C. 1 Cor. 5:11 (NIV) gives us a similar list of things that are obviously inappropriate for a child of God—those who are sexually immoral, greedy, etc.

But now I am writing you that you must not associate with anyone who calls himself a brother but is sexually immoral or greedy, an idolater or a slanderer, a drunkard or a swindler. With such a man do not even eat.

D. 1 Cor. 6:9-10 (NIV) *Do you not know that the wicked will not inherit the kingdom of God? Do not be deceived: Neither the sexually immoral nor idolaters nor adulterers nor male prostitutes nor homosexual offenders 10 nor thieves nor the greedy nor drunkards nor slanderers nor swindlers will inherit the kingdom of God.*

3. Exclude people with divisive spirit and bind on others what they believe.

A. 3 Jn. 1:9-10 (NIV) *I wrote to the church, but Diotrephes, who loves to be first, will have nothing to do with us. So if I come, I will call attention to what he is doing, gossiping maliciously about us. Not satisfied with that, he refuses to welcome the brothers. He also stops those who want to do so and puts them out of the church.*

B. Rom. 1:16-17 (NIV) The theme of Romans is revealed here:

I am not ashamed of the gospel, because it is the power of God for the salvation of everyone who believes: first for the Jew, then for the Gentile. For in the gospel a righteousness from God is revealed, a righteousness that is by faith from first to last, just as it is written: "The righteous will live by faith."

The rest of Romans expands upon that theme that we are saved by grace through faith and not by works. Those who are requiring circumcision and the following of legalistic rules are causing divisions and putting obstacles in the way of the followers. About them Paul says in Rom. 16:17 (NIV)

I urge you, brothers, to watch out for those who cause divisions and put obstacles in your way that are contrary to the teaching you have learned. Keep away from them.

This one is a little scary to me, this binding on others what I believe—especially the legalistic rules part. It should make us very cautious about what we demand from others before we accept them as brothers. It should also make us very cautious about rejecting others who truly do believe in Christ. It cuts both ways.

C. Tit. 3:9-10 (NIV) *But avoid foolish controversies and genealogies and arguments and quarrels about the law, because these are unprofitable and useless. Warn a divisive person once, and then warn him a second time. After that, have nothing to do with him.*

D. Tit. 1:10-11 (NIV) *For there are many rebellious people, mere talkers and deceivers, especially those of the circumcision group. They must be silenced, because they are ruining whole households by teaching things they ought not to teach—and that for the sake of dishonest gain.*

4. Exclude a brother who refuses correction after biblical procedures.

> **Matt. 18:15-17 (NIV)** *If your brother sins against you, go and show him his fault, just between the two of you. If he listens to you, you have won your brother over. But if he will not listen, take one or two others along, so that 'every matter may be established by the testimony of two or three witnesses.' If he refuses to listen to them, tell it to the church; and if he refuses to listen even to the church, treat him as you would a pagan or a tax collector.*

These are the specific examples we are given in the New Testament for rejecting people from the church. Do we have any biblical justification for excluding anyone from the church who does **not** fall into one of these very clear and specific categories? I do not think so. These are the only Biblical examples I could find that authorized the exclusion of people who had become Christians at one time. This leads me to my next question:

Have we ever excluded anyone for any reason other than those specifically authorized above?

Unfortunately, for me personally, my answer has to be, ***"Yes, Lord, I have. Please forgive me."***

But now we have a dilemma. Many scriptures talk about "contending for the faith," fighting "false teachers," and "false doctrine." What about all of these issues? Do they authorize us to exclude those who are guilty of teaching error? These are good and legitimate questions. Let us address them now.

Contending for the Faith

The question we will discuss now has to do with those people who did not fall into the "authorized kick out" categories but are, nevertheless, not full of "sound doctrine" or are "false teachers." Are they still our brothers in spite of their faulty doctrine or false teaching? Let us look at false teachers in the Bible to see who and what was included in those descriptions.

When I was growing up there was a widely accepted publication called *Contending for the Faith*. Written in the heading area was a statement that it was "for, elders, preachers, teachers and concerned Christians," that it "was begun and continues to exist to **defend the gospel** (Phil. 1:7, 17) and **refute error** (Jude 3)."

These are good and biblical causes—**"defending the gospel,"** and **"refuting error."** Paul states *for whether I am in chains or defending and confirming the gospel, all of you share in God's grace with me* (Phil. 1:7 NIV).

As I was growing up in my biblical training, I very often heard this "contending for the faith," "defending the gospel" and other, similar sounding phrases.

Generally speaking, many—including me—have used one or more of these phrases to justify condemning anyone who did not agree with what was believed and accepted about instrumental music, the name on the building, how often to take communion, baptism, etc. This "Contending for the Faith" publication has used the phrase in much the same way.

But what is the "gospel" of which these verses speak? Is it not the "good news:" that Jesus came and died for our sins, and that he was buried and rose again, that we might have eternal life? Yes! That is the gospel.

And sometimes we may need reminding, like those Christians needed in 1 Cor. 15:1-8, about what was of "first importance." And we, as members of his body, should indeed defend the gospel. We should not allow it to be taught that any of this did not happen or that Jesus was not the son of God. **But these verses do not give us the right to condemn everyone with whom we disagree on every doctrinal issue**. It is just not in the scriptures.

In Jude 3, from which the publication takes its name, Christ's followers were urged to "**contend for the faith** that was once for all entrusted to the saints."

As we continue on into verse 4, we see what the writer was telling them to contend: against *certain men whose condemnation was written about long ago have secretly slipped in among you. They are godless men, who change the grace of our God into a license for immorality and deny Jesus Christ our only Sovereign and Lord.*

I encourage you to read the rest of Jude to see how vile and worldly these men were. They met both of the criteria that we studied earlier; they were extremely immoral, and they denied Jesus as the only Sovereign and Lord.

If we have men among us who deny Jesus and are immoral, we should not tolerate their presence for a moment. I am in total agreement with "Contending for the Faith" to this point. I am in disagreement when it condemns others for every doctrinal issue.

But what about **false teachers and their false doctrine** that is different than the specific examples mentioned in those passages? Let us take a look at that.

False Teachers and Doctrine

Let us look at some of the other verses we have used to justify our exclusion of others. For example:

2 Jn. 9-11 (NIV) *anyone who does not continue in the teaching of Christ does not have God; whoever continues in the teaching has both the Father and the Son. If anyone comes to you and does not bring this teaching, do not take him into your house or welcome him. Anyone who welcomes him shares in his wicked work.*

We have traditionally used this passage to cover many subjects and issues. But, if you look back to verse seven, you will see that he is talking to them about *Many deceivers, who do not acknowledge Jesus Christ as coming in the flesh, [and who] have gone out into the world. Any such person is the deceiver and the antichrist.* It is back to the basics of "first importance" in 1 Cor. 15.

Gal 1:8 (NIV) *. . . preach a different gospel than the one we preached to you, let him be eternally condemned.* We have had the tendency to expand this to mean everything we believe, not just the gospel. Once again, we need to keep in mind 1 Cor. 15:1-8, the heart of the gospel, and confine our condemning to those who violate that principle.

Phil. 3:17b-18 (NIV) *take note of those who live according to the pattern we gave you for, as I have often told you . . .many live as enemies of the cross of Christ.*

Verse 2 tells who he is talking about—*those dogs, those men who do evil, those mutilators of the flesh.*

These were men of the circumcision party who were trying to force people to be circumcised before they would be accepted as brothers. There seemed to be other problems as well: v19 *...their god is their stomach, and their glory is in their shame. Their mind is on earthly things.*

This passage does not, on the one hand, give us license to attack everyone who disagrees with us on some doctrinal issues, but is, on the other hand, very specific about the person it should be used against.

1 Tim 1:3 (NIV) *. . . command certain men not to teach false doctrines any longer.*

What did Paul specifically mean when he wrote about "false doctrines" in this situation. In the verses following this instruction, he spelled out some examples of what he meant.

V4 not to devote themselves to myths and endless genealogies. These promote controversies rather than God's work—which is by faith.

V7 they want to be teachers of the law, but do not know what they are talking about...the law is made for lawbreakers and rebels, the ungodly and sinful, the unholy and irreligious; for those who kill their fathers or mothers, for murderers, for adulterers and perverts, for slave traders and liars and perjurers—and for whatever else is contrary to the sound doctrine that conforms to the glorious gospel of the blessed God,....

These examples of "false doctrine" are quite different from the examples that have frequently been labeled "false doctrines" by members of the Church of Christ. Perhaps we should restrain ourselves when tempted to use this verse to condemn everyone who disagrees with us.

1 Tim 6:3-4 (NIV) *If anyone teaches false doctrines and does not agree to the sound instruction of our Lord Jesus Christ and to godly teaching he is conceited and understands nothing.*

Paul follows this statement, in the second half of verse 4, with a description of such a false teacher.

... he has an unhealthy interest in controversies and quarrels about words that result in envy, strife, malicious talk, evil suspicions and constant friction between men of corrupt mind, who have been robbed of the truth and who think that godliness is a means to financial gain.

Need I say more?

1 Tim 4:1 (NIV) *The Spirit clearly says that in later times some will abandon the faith and follow deceiving spirits and things taught by demons. Such teachings come through hypocritical liars, who consciences have been seared as with a hot iron.*

Just what are these things being taught by these hypocritical liars?

They forbid people to marry and order them to abstain from certain foods, which God created to be received with thanksgiving.

And, when he was writing to Titus, Paul told him to appoint elders in every town, describing the kind of man Titus was to look for. As part of that description, Paul told Titus that *He must hold firmly to the trustworthy message as it has been taught, so that he can encourage others by sound doctrine and refute those who oppose it (Tit. 1:9).*

Paul then explains why he gave this instruction (there is a practical reason for all of God's instructions).

1 Tim 4:10 (NIV) *For there are many rebellious people, mere talkers and deceivers, especially those of the circumcision group. They must be silenced, because they are ruining whole households by teaching things they ought not to teach—and that for the sake of dishonest gain. Even one of their own prophets has said, 'Cretans are always liars, evil brutes, lazy gluttons.' This testimony is true. Therefore, rebuke them sharply, so that they will be sound in the faith and will pay no attention to Jewish myths or to the commands of those who reject the truth. . . . They claim to know God, but by their actions they deny him. They are detestable, disobedient and unfit for doing anything good.*

Beginning with the next chapter, Paul then tells Titus, *You must teach what is in accord with sound doctrine* (**Tit. 2:1 (NIV)**, followed by a description of what that is. It is significantly different than what we have traditionally viewed as being a part of "sound doctrine."

Tit. 2:2-15 (NIV) *Teach the older men to be temperate, worthy of respect, self-controlled, and sound in faith, in love and in endurance. Likewise, teach the older women to be reverent in the way they live, not to be slanderers or addicted to much wine, but to teach what is good. Then they can train the younger women to love their husbands and children, to be self-controlled and pure, to be busy at home, to be kind, and to be subject to their husbands, so that no one will malign the word of God. Similarly, encourage the young men to be self-controlled. In everything set them an example by doing what is good. In your teaching show integrity, seriousness and soundness of speech that cannot be condemned, so that those who oppose you may be ashamed because they have nothing bad to say about us. Teach slaves to be subject to their masters in everything, to try to please them, not to talk back to them, and not to steal from them, but to show that they can be fully trusted, so that in every way they will make the teaching about God our Savior attractive. For the grace of God that brings salvation has appeared to all men. It teaches us to say "No" to ungodliness and worldly passions, and to live self-controlled, upright and godly lives in this present age, while we wait for the blessed hope—the glorious appearing of our great God and Savior, Jesus Christ, who gave himself for us to redeem us from all wickedness and to purify for himself a people that are his very own, eager to do what is good. These, then, are the things you should teach. Encourage and rebuke with all authority. Do not let anyone despise you.*

2 Pet 2:1,13-14 (NIV). *. . . there will be false teachers among you. (They will secretly introduce destructive heresies, even denying the sovereign Lord who brought them. . . . Their idea of pleasure is to carouse in broad daylight. With eyes full of adultery, they never stop sinning; they seduce the unstable; they are experts in greed . . ..)*

To summarize, there is responsibility on our part to refute false teachings and false teachers and to teach sound doctrine. That is undeniable. I have no problem with it.

Where I have a concern is in my belief that often we have expanded the parameters of what that term, "false teaching," encompasses. Now that we have a better understanding, we should refrain from using it for everything that disagrees with our understanding of God's Word.

Summary of False Teachers

It seems that, generally speaking, the false teachers spoken about in the New Testament primarily fit into one or more of the following categories. They were men:

> **1)** whose hearts and motives were not trying to serve God but, instead, were trying to mislead people for personal gain,
>
> **2)** who wanted no restrictions on their lives or moral actions,
>
> **3)** who were trying to bind their beliefs and opinions on other people, and
>
> **4)** who denied the heart of the Gospel (For a quick reminder see 1 Cor. 15:1-8).

Fruit Inspectors

Some have mentioned that we are to be "fruit inspectors," that we should watch out for false teachers by watching for their bad fruits. *By their fruit you shall recognize them* **(Lk 6:44; Matt. 7:15-20)**. And we should use this to determine who is my brother [as well as the methods we have mentioned in the previous lessons].

Let us look a little deeper into this "fruit inspection" policy, according to the Bible.

These references to good and bad fruit are recorded in Matthew, Luke and John. Let us explore each of them to see what was said and then examine the context in which they were written.

Matt. 3:8,10 (NIV) *Produce fruit in keeping with repentance... every tree that does not produce good fruit will be cut down and thrown into the fire.*

This statement was made by John the Baptist, while in the desert near the Jordan river. He was baptizing people who came to him confessing their sins. When he saw the Pharisees and Sadducees coming, he called them a "brood of vipers," because they did not feel the need to repent, since they were descendents of Abraham. Anyone who does not repent of his sins cannot bear the fruit about which John is speaking.

Matt. 7:15-16 (NIV) *Watch out for false prophets... By their fruit you will recognize them.... Every good tree bears good fruit, but a bad tree bears bad fruit.... Every tree that does not bear good fruit is cut down and thrown into the fire. Thus, by their fruit you will recognize them.*

This is Jesus' statement in his Sermon on the Mount. In the second half of verse 15, Jesus more fully describes these false prophets. *They come to you in sheep's clothing, but inwardly they are ferocious wolves.*

These are not men having pure hearts but limited understanding. They are aggressors who intentionally mislead and destroy the vulnerable.

Matt. 12:33 (NIV) *Make a tree good and its fruit will be good, or make a tree bad and its fruit will be bad, for a tree is recognized by its fruit.*

Jesus made this statement to the Pharisees after he had driven a demon out of a man. The Pharisees were saying that Jesus had done this by Beelzebub. In verse 34 Jesus calls them a *"brood of vipers."* He then calls them evil, saying that evil things come out of their mouths because of the evil stored up in their hearts.

Once again, these are not good people who need further teaching; they are evil men who would like to destroy Jesus.

> **Lk. 3:8,9 (NIV)** *Produce fruit in keeping with repentance. . . . The ax is already at the root of the trees, and every tree that does not produce good fruit will be cut down and thrown into the fire.*

This is Luke's account of the same Matthew 3 incident. After the people heard John call the Pharisees a "brood of vipers," they asked him (in verse 10), *What should we do then?* John replied in the next 4 verses with a list of "good fruit" examples.

> **Lk. 3:11, 13, 14 (NIV)** *The man with two tunics should share with him who has none, and the one who has food should do the same.. ...And to the tax collectors who were baptized, do not collect any more than you are required to. And to the soldiers who were baptized do not extort money and do not accuse people falsely—be content with your pay.*

These are not exactly the same kinds of things we have used to differentiate between good fruit and bad fruit in the church.

> **Lk. 6:43, 45 (NIV)** *No good tree bears bad fruit, nor does a bad tree bear good fruit. Each tree is recognized by its own fruit. People do not pick figs from thornbushes, or grapes from briers.*

This comes from Luke's account of Jesus' sermon on the mount. He follows these verses with a fuller description of the kind of people he's talking about.

> *The good man brings good things out of the good stored up in his heart, and the evil man brings evil things out of the evil stored up in his heart. For out of the overflow of his heart his mouth speaks.*

Once again we are talking about evil hearts, not pure hearts who are mistaken.

For us to use these verses to condemn people who are searching for the truth, but come to different conclusions than do we, is a misuse of the scriptures.

But what about those people who are sincere, but are sadly mistaken in their understanding of God's will? **Does accepting them, in effect, cause us to condone doctrinal error?**

That is another great question. Let's find out.

Wrong, but Still "Innies"

1. The Weak Brother

In 1 Cor. 8, Paul is addressing the Corinthians about the doctrinal issue (yes, it was very much a doctrinal issue) of eating meat offered to idols.

After a reading of verses 4-8, it becomes clear that, doctrinally speaking, **there is nothing wrong, in and of itself, with eating meat offered to idols.** This means that, **those who believed that it was wrong to eat this meat were in doctrinal error.** In a real sense, they were believing and teaching false doctrine.

And yet, Paul treated them very differently from those he treated who were teaching false doctrine in the scriptures we studied previously. Why is that?

Could it be that even though their understanding of God's Word was wrong, their motives were right? They were abstaining from eating meat because of their faith in Christ.

And, though they were wrong, what they believed did not deny the heart of the gospel. Nor did they believe it for selfish gain. Their belief did not cause them to live blatantly immoral lives.

They were Christians who misunderstood God's Word and, consequently, were living out what they believed to be sound doctrine. Because of that, Paul just called them "weak brothers," not "false teachers." Should we do any differently?

Paul gives similar instructions in Romans 14:1,5,13 when he is writing about how some brothers eat meat while others eat vegetables only. At the same time he writes about how various brothers disagree about whether or not one day is more sacred than others.

He tells them, and us, to *accept him whose faith is weak, without passing judgment on disputable matters.* Then he reiterates, *Stop passing judgment on one another. Instead, make up your mind not to put any stumbling block or obstacle in your brother's way.*

2. Worldly—Mere Infants in Christ

In 1 Cor. 3, Paul was dealing with another issue—following after different men in the church.

Keep in mind that, even though these believers are following after different men, and are jealous and quarrelsome (v3), Paul still calls them brothers (v1). Previously, he had called them *the church of God...those sanctified in Christ Jesus and called to be holy...*, and then shortly thereafter he begins talking to them about their divisions.

When he gets to chapter 3 verse 1, he does not call them "false teachers," but *worldly—mere infants in Christ*.

Why does he not call them false teachers? In verses 16-17 he tells them that *God's temple is sacred, and you are that temple*.

Once again, though they were wrong, what they believed did not deny the heart of the gospel. Nor did they believe it for selfish gain. Their belief did not cause them to live blatantly immoral lives.

They were believers who misunderstood God's Word, who were living out what they believed to be sound doctrine. Because of that, Paul just called them *worldly—mere infants in Christ.*

But what if they never grow up? I believe Paul deals with that in this same chapter. Let us look at what he has to say.

3. Gold or Straw

Look at 1 Cor. 3:10-15. Paul discusses the work that he and Apollos and Cephas are doing. He talks about how their work must be laid on the foundation that Jesus Christ laid and no other.

He talks about how some men will build on this foundation using gold, silver, costly stones, wood, hay or straw (v12).

He then tells of how each man's work will be tested. *It will be revealed with fire, and the fire will test the quality of each man's work. If what he has built survives, he will receive his reward. If it is burned up, he will suffer loss: he himself will be saved, but only as one escaping through the flames. (1 Cor 2:13-15 NIV)*

If I correctly understand this illustration, Paul, Apollos and Cephas are the workers and these Christians are their work. In the final judgment, some of these converts may be burned up as if they are wood, hay or straw as opposed to gold, silver or costly stones. It seems that this is determined by the kind of lives they lead.

At what point is that determination made? It does not say specifically, but there may not be a determination until judgment day. At that point, God will decide.

Until that point, I believe it is my responsibility to love and accept those converts (Rom 14:1) and consider them brothers, unless they violate one of the key principles that we talked about earlier.

It is also my responsibility to try, in love, to teach them and encourage them—to make sure they are made of gold.

Summary

Paul calls them the church of God (1 Cor 1:2, Rom. 1:7) even though

    A. They are worldly, infants in Christ   1 Cor 3:1

    B. They are jealous and quarrelsome   1 Cor 3:3

    C. They are following different men   1 Cor 1:11-13, 3:4-5

    D. They disagree about eating meat from idols   Rom 4:2

    E. They disagree about what days are sacred   Rom 14:5

Conclusion

1. So how should we treat those with whom we disagree?

A. We should not allow ourselves to be bound by a legalistic set of rules.

Gal 5:1,13 (NIV) *It is for freedom that Christ has set us free. Stand firm, then, and do not let yourselves be burdened again by a yoke of slavery....do not use your freedom to indulge in the sinful nature; rather, serve one another in love.*

B. We should be tolerant of those with different views and beliefs.

Eph. 4:2 (NIV) *Be completely humble and gentle; be patient, bearing with one another in love. Make every effort to keep the unity of the Spirit through the bond of peace.*

Rom. 14:1-13 (NIV) *Accept him whose faith is weak, without passing judgment on disputable matters. . . . Who are you to judge someone else's servant? To his own master he stands or falls. . . You, then, why do you judge your brother? Or why do you look down on your brother? For we will all stand before God's judgment seat. 12 So then, each of us will give an account of himself to God. . . . Therefore let us stop passing judgment on one another.*

Rom.15:1-7 (NIV) *We who are strong ought to bear with the failings of the weak . . . . May the God who gives endurance and encouragement give you a spirit of unity among yourselves as you follow Christ Jesus, so that with one heart and mouth you may glorify the God and Father of our Lord Jesus Christ. Accept one another, then, just as Christ accepted you, in order to bring praise to God.*

2. Keep in fellowship when

A. They are spiritual babes —Rom. 14:1 (they need it to help them grow).

B. They are snared by sin (They need it to bring them back).

C. They have unorthodox views (that do not deny the gospel, for the sake of teaching, encouraging, and rescue from harm).*

In considering how we should act toward our brothers with whom we have differences, we should continue to study together, to more perfectly understand what God's will is for us. As long as we are continuing to strive to be what God wants us to be, we must continue to consider ourselves brothers.

It is entirely possible that we could be as wrong in our understanding of God's word as we assume our brothers to be. But so long as neither of us wrecks our faith by denying the heart of the gospel or by living blatantly immoral lives, then surely we are brothers.

If we do not accept them, we may be rejecting someone whom God has accepted. I do not want to risk that. May God bless us as we try to understand his will.

PLEASE NOTE: I have tried my best not to plagiarize the work of others in the writing of this book. That said, I have been influenced so much by so many Godly men and women through the decades that sometimes sources for inspiration and/or information sort of run together.

A little tiny voice in my brain tells me that I first heard this Part 2, A, B and C (on the previous page) in 1970 or 71 when I was taking notes during a sermon by an awesome Biblical scholar, Dr. Raymond Kelcy, when I was a student at Oklahoma Christian College.

Whether I actually did hear it from him or not, I'm just not sure, but I can attest without hesitation that he, as well as many others, like Dr. Hugo McCord, Cecil Hook, John McCarther and others were a profound influence on my understanding of, and approach to scripture. I thank God for these and many other men and women who have influenced me over the years. My deepest apologies if/when I do not give them credit for the good they have done in my life and in this book.

Understanding God's Will

Introduction

Multiple Interpretation Methods

We, in the Church of Christ, have been using multiple methods of Bible interpretation to come to our doctrinal conclusions. We do not use the same method for each topic. We use one method for some topics, and another method for other topics.

This is a foreign concept to most people in the Church of Christ, because most of us have been doing it without ever realizing it. The first time I mention this concept of multiple interpretations to my Christian friends, they usually get a puzzled look on their faces and say, "What do you mean?"

What I mean is, we have been using multiple methods of Bible interpretation to come to our doctrinal conclusions.

It took me forty or fifty years to realize that this is what we have been doing. Eventually, I also came to realize that a high percentage of our Bible class time is dedicated, not to actually studying the Bible for the purpose of understanding what it means, but for the purpose of memorizing which method of interpretation should be applied to each topic.

If we use the "wrong" method of interpretation for a topic, our conclusions will likely come out different, i.e., wrong! Therefore, it has been important for us to make sure that we learn the right methods.

What has led to the presence of two or three different Churches of Christ in most every small Bible Belt town is the choice of the brethren in each church to use a different method of interpretation for the various topics under consideration.

I know it seems a little confusing at first, but I think you will agree with what I am saying after you hear more of what I have to say.

I put together a series, "Understanding God's Will," to encourage us to rethink what God wants from us—to challenge some of our long-held beliefs and to attempt to get us to a more Biblically-correct place.

Let us examine some of the methods we've used in the past to understand God's will, and see the effect they have had on us.

Method # 1

God Means What He Says!

We have traditionally used a few scriptures to prove that God "means what he says." These verses give us much comfort and confidence if we take a legalistic view of God's Word. They seem to have a very cut and dried, black and white, undeniable message for us today. And that message is, "Do exactly what God says—or else." Following are some examples of scriptures we have used to prove our point:

A. Touching the Ark of the Covenant

1.) **1 Chron. 13:9-10 (NIV)** *...Uzzah reached out his hand to steady the ark, because the oxen stumbled. The Lord's anger burned against Uzzah, and he struck him down because he had put his hand on the ark. So he died there before God.*

Two chapters later we find out what, specifically, caused Uzzah's death when he touched the ark.

2.) **1 Chron.15:2,12,13 (NIV)**...*you and your fellow **Levites are to consecrate yourselves** and bring up the ark of the Lord, the God of Israel, to the place I have prepared for it.* ***It was because you, the Levites, did not bring it up the first time that the Lord our God broke out in anger against us.*** *We did not inquire of him about how to do it in the prescribed way.*

In Exodus, we see the specific way in which God had commanded the ark to be carried, different from what had been tried when Uzzah died.

3.) Ex. 27:7 (NIV) *The poles are to be inserted into the rings so they will be on two sides of the alter when it is carried.* (This instruction is repeated in Ex. 25:14)

B. Annanias and Saphira

1.) Ex.20:16 (NIV) *You shall not bear false witness against your neighbor*

2.) Lev 19:11 (NIV) *Do not lie. Do not deceive one another.*

3.) Acts 5:1-11 (NIV) Annanias and Saphira sold their land as an offering to the Lord; but they conspired to hold back part of the money they had received and to lie about it. Because of this, they were struck dead at the altar.

C. Remembering the Sabbath

1.) Ex. 31:14-15 (NIV) *Observe the Sabbath, because it is holy to you. Anyone who desecrates it must be put to death;*

2.) Exodus 20:8-10 (NIV) *Remember the Sabbath day by keeping it holy. Six days you shall labor and do all your work, but the seventh day is a Sabbath to the LORD your God. On it you shall not do any work, neither you, nor your son or daughter, nor your manservant or maidservant, nor your animals, nor the alien within your gates.*

3.) Jeremiah 17:21-22 (NIV) *This is what the LORD says: Be careful not to carry a load on the Sabbath day or bring it through the gates of Jerusalem. Do not bring a load out of your houses or do any work on the Sabbath, but keep the Sabbath day holy, as I commanded your forefathers.*

4.) Exodus 35:2 (NIV) *For six days, work is to be done, but the seventh day shall be your holy day, a Sabbath of rest to the LORD. Whoever does any work on it must be put to death.*

    a. Violation–Numbers 15:32-36, A man was found gathering wood on the Sabbath. The Lord told Moses, *The man must die. The whole assembly must stone him outside the camp.* So they stoned him to death.

b. Violation–Ex. 16:26 God told the people to gather manna six days but not on Sabbath. Some people went out on the Sabbath anyway, but they found no manna.

Following these examples, we say something to the effect that "God means what he says and when we fail to follow his commands completely, we are condemned—without exception."

We then launch into a discussion about instrumental music. When God said to sing and make melody in your heart, he meant "sing." Any other action or addition to this action is the same as using some wood other than gopher wood to build the ark (which does not really prove anything that I can tell, since we do not know what would have happened if Noah had used some other wood).

And any other action or addition to this command is the same as if we would have gathered wood on the Sabbath. Anyone who does it is in violation of God's Word and will be condemned.

If you preach a sermon like this, based upon the given information, you have the more conservative-minded believers sitting on the edge of their seats filled with "joy" and shouting their "Amen" while condemning instrumental music, clapping, and other activities. This is definitely in their comfort zone, and a mountain-top experience.

In fact, I have never seen them more in their comfort zone than at that moment in that particular sermon on that particular topic. That has kind of been a Super Bowl sermon.

I have felt that same feeling of joy and exultation at that very same moment myself, many times. It is a favorite, for sure. So, I understand, from a very personal point of view, what a glorious moment it is.

The only problem is, the reasoning is flawed. The scriptures included in the sermon do not look at the whole picture. In addition to the previous examples, where violations resulted in severe punishment, there were also several times in the Bible when people violated those same commands and did not reap the same punishment as did the people in those examples.

In fact, sometimes they violated these commands with positive results. And yet, these exceptions are *never* mentioned by the person or the preacher who is trying to prove the sinfulness of instrumental music. To do so would cloud the issue.

So what should we do? **Should we continue to leave out the passages that would weaken our arguments?** Or should be go back to the scriptures to see if what we have been saying needs a little tweaking?

Let us look at some of the exceptions I just mentioned as we begin to put together some of the pieces of the puzzle to learn how to interpret God's Word more correctly.

Exceptions

A. Yes, Annanias and Saphira lied and died, but

1. Josh. 2:1-7 (NIV) Rahab the Harlot lied as she hid Joshua's two spies. Because of what she did, welcoming the spies and lying about having them, she is listed with the heroes of faith.

2. Heb. 11:31 (NIV) *By faith the prostitute Rahab, because she welcomed the spies, was not killed with those who were disobedient.*

B. Yes, God said, "Do no work on the Sabbath," but,

    1. Lk. 13:10, Mk. 3:1-6 Jesus healed on the Sabbath.

    2. Mk. 2:23-28 Jesus and disciples picked grain on Sabbath. Jesus response to his critics was that *Sabbath is made for man–not man for Sabbath.* What? What does that say to us who have used the Sabbath principle to condemn people for using a piano? Maybe this argument is not quite as cut and dried as we thought.

C. Yes, God said, about eating the bread of the presence,

    1. Lev. 24:9 It is to be eaten only by the priests.

    Lev. 24:8-9 (NIV) *This bread is to be set out before the LORD regularly, Sabbath after Sabbath, on behalf of the Israelites, as a lasting covenant. It belongs to Aaron and his sons, who are to eat it in a holy place, because it is a most holy part of their regular share of the offerings made to the LORD by fire.*

    2. 1 Sam 21:4 But, David, who definitely was not a priest, ate this bread when he was at Nob, running from Saul. He experienced no ill effects from eating this bread.

    3. Jesus uses David's incident, as well as the picking grain on the Sabbath incident to illustrate the principle that the ceremonial law was not to be viewed in a legalistic manner. Read the account below.

    Mk. 2:23-28 (NIV) *One Sabbath Jesus was going through the grainfields, and as his disciples walked along, they began to pick some heads of grain. The Pharisees said* *to him, "Look, why are they doing what is unlawful on the Sabbath?" He answered, "Have you never read what David did when he and his companions were hungry and in need? In the days of Abiathar the high priest, he entered the house of God and ate the consecrated bread, which is lawful only for priests to eat. And he also gave some to his companions." Then he said to them, "The Sabbath was made for man, not man for the Sabbath. So the Son of Man is Lord even of the Sabbath.*

This is very much in keeping with the big picture principle that we find in **Hosea 6:6 (NIV)** where God says, *For I desire mercy, not sacrifice, and acknowledgment of God rather than burnt offerings.*

D. Woman caught in adultery

    1. Deut 22:23-24; Lev 20:10 If a man or woman were caught in adultery, they were to be put to death. That is crystal clear. Right?

    2. Jn. 8:7 A woman who had been caught in adultery was brought before Jesus.

    3. Jn. 8:11 He did not condemn her.

So what are we to conclude from these scriptures? Are they sending mixed messages? Why is there such a difference in the consequences for these various acts of disobedience?

Traditionally, we have used some of these verses in the first half of this discussion to justify our condemnation of others, but when we look at all of them together, it seems that we may have been over anxious in our condemnation.

It seems that we have had a tendency to pick out the verses that justify what we want to do or say. We should have been looking at all the verses to try to find out how God wants us to be.

Of course, God wants our obedience. I am not saying he does not. Of course he does. But I believe that we have sometimes heard a different message than the one he is sending.

Real proof of this is in Micah 6:6-8 where it appears that God is not satisfied with what *he* specifically asked for.

Mic. 6:6-8 (NIV) *With what shall I come before the LORD and bow down before the exalted God? Shall I come before him with burnt offerings, with calves a year old? Will the LORD be pleased with thousands of rams, with ten thousand rivers of oil? Shall I offer my firstborn for my transgression, the fruit of my body for the sin of my soul? He has showed you, O man, what is good. And what does the LORD require of you? To act justly and to love mercy and to walk humbly with your God.*

It is clear that even if we get every detail right, but have the wrong attitude and mindset, then it is not pleasing to God.

More than our obedience, doesn't he desire our hearts? **(Heb. 10:22 (NIV)** *let us draw near to God with a sincere heart in full assurance of faith,*) We'll talk more about this later.

Carefully consider the following case as it deals with God's commands.

Greet One Another with a Holy Kiss

God commanded Noah to build an ark. He told Noah specifically to use gopher wood and gave him the exact dimensions to build the ark. If Noah had, in full faith and sincerity, used a wood other than gopher wood, would he have been obeying God? If he had built the ark different from those specifications God gave, would he have been obeying God? If God specified gopher wood, did Noah know that no other wood was allowed, or did God have to list all the trees of the forest not to use? Do we want to be guilty today of building the church with a worship God did not prescribe?

Nadab and Abihu, the sons of Aaron, offered "strange fire" before the Lord, fire which He had not authorized: If they were sincerely and honestly presenting their offering, would that have been enough to make the offering acceptable to God? If God had specified a source (Leviticus 6:12, 13; 16:12; Numbers 16:46), did His specification necessarily exclude all other sources of fire? Do we want to be guilty today of offering "strange worship" to God, worship that He has not authorized?

Zacharias, in Luke 1:13, was commanded to name his son "John." Did the angel have to tell him all the names *not* to name the child for him to know it must be "John"? In fact, for doubting the angel, he was punished with muteness until the correct name was given. Mary was commanded to name her son "Jesus." Did the angel have to list all the other names for her to know that no other name was acceptable?

The New Testament clearly authorizes us to greet one another with a holy kiss. If God had simply said to "greet one another" but not specified *how* to greet one another, we would be free to greet any way we chose, just as Noah would have been free to build the ark of any wood he chose and as Nadab and Abihu could have offered any fire they chose, and as Zacharias and Mary could have named their boys any name they chose. But God has specified *how* to greet one another in the church.

I know that you are familiar with the Scriptures that teach this. Since God specified *how* to greet one another, it necessarily implies that we are not to greet one another in any other way, just as it was necessarily implied that Noah was not to build the ark with any other wood. God did not need to make a list of all the trees in the world of which Noah was not to build the ark.

He did not need to make a list of all the kinds of fire in the world from which the priests were not to make offerings. He did not need to list all the names not to give to John and Jesus. His specification of exactly what He wanted, and silence on everything else, implied that anything other than what He specified was *not* acceptable.

Likewise, God does not need to make a list of all the ways in which we are not to greet one another for us to understand that the church is to greet with a holy kiss. God has specified greeting with a holy kiss for the church, and shaking hands is not a holy kiss.

Greeting with a holy kiss is acceptable to God in the church. Hand-shaking is not a holy kiss any more than sprinkling is immersing. That person shaking hands might be sincere and honestly trying to greet, but hand-shaking is not a holy kiss. The New Testament authorizes holy kissing, not shaking hands, and shaking hands is not holy kissing!

He said to *greet with a holy kiss,* necessarily implying that anything different from holy kissing was excluded. And shaking hands is not holy kissing!

But, let us assume for a moment that hand-shaking is acceptable. If we can shake hands, then can we "high five"? If we can high five, can we knock our knuckles? Can we wink and nod? Can we twang on our mustaches? Can we bump our chests? Can we put our hands under our armpits and make squelching sounds? After all, we are still greeting, are we not?

Where will we draw the line? How far can we go before we realize that those things are not authorized ways of greeting? Obviously, when we open the door to shaking of hands, we have to let in a lot of other things, too.

Hand-shaking is not the safest, surest way to greet one another, because the Scripture is silent on it. Are we going to practice what we can prove with book, chapter, and verse, or what we cannot safely and surely prove with Scriptures?

We have said that we should do that which is safest and surest, staying away from questionable practices that take us closer to the edge of sin rather than keeping us straight down the middle of the path that leads to salvation.

If you have ever read or watched a debate or trial, you know that the burden of proof lies with the person affirming it. In other words, the person who claims something to be true or acceptable must prove it; the person denying it can win the debate or trial without even saying a word if the person affirming fails to prove conclusively.

I can affirm and prove that greeting with a holy kiss is authorized in the church, and I am sure you would not disagree with me.

But if you want to affirm that hand-shaking is authorized in the church, you have the burden of proof. You must produce evidence from the Scriptures that the New Testament churches did it. You must prove it true and acceptable to God. If your only justification and proof is that the Scripture does not say not to do it, your case is lost.

Restoration-era preacher J.W. McGarvey said, "We cannot, therefore, by any possibility, know that a certain element of worship is acceptable to God in the Christian dispensation, when the Scriptures which speak of that dispensation are silent in reference to it. To introduce any such element is unscriptural and presumptuous." (Millenial Harbinger, 1864, pp. 511-513).

Moses Lard said, "In all acts of worship we must do only what is prescribed in the New Testament, or was done with divine sanction by the primitive Christians. Not the semblance of innovation must be allowed on this sacred principle" (Lard's Quarterly, Vol. 4, p. 395).

In my Bible's footnote regarding Rom. 16:16 it says that Justin Martyr (an early historian) [A.D. 150] tells us that "the holy kiss was a regular part of the worship service in his day." Can there be any denying that this is what the Lord commanded and that this was the practice of the early Christians?

I hope that you will consider all of this. Hand-shaking is "strange fire" which the Lord has not authorized. Hand-shaking is a wood other than the gopher wood Noah used. Hand-shaking is not holy kissing. Hand-shaking is no different from using mechanical instruments, and I will have nothing to do with that!

Note: This argument is used to prove that we are authorized (and even commanded) to "sing" (two times), and that we are not authorized to clap or use an instrument or any other "noise maker" in our worship—and that to do so would be sinful.

My goal in making the case for Holy kissing is to illustrate what happens when we substitute another command, that God gave, five clear and specific times, into this method of interpretation. Using the exact same arguments in the exact same way seems to demand the same type of conclusions—that holy kissing is the only authorized method of greeting.

And yet, we have not chosen to follow this interpretation on this particular command. I would like to make clear to all my readers that I personally believe that this method of interpretation is flawed, that it brings one to conclusions that God never intended—like it is wrong to shake hands.

For the record, I think shaking hands is perfectly fine with God. I do not think the point of the command is to be so legalistic as to interpret it as I have illustrated it above. Nor do I think we should use it to interpret "sing" in the way that we have.

My purpose is neither to make fun of anyone or to make anyone mad but to make people think and to stop binding things that are not meant to be bound.

I do not want to be like the Pharisees who tried to require circumcision and the celebration of "special days" and feasts before they would accept others as brothers. If you have been angered or felt disrespected, I apologize. That is not my purpose.

I hope you will consider it possible that we have been legalistic in our "God Means What He Says" approach to Bible study. It is possible that we have convicted others unjustly. Please consider.

Method # 2
Custom vs Command

There are several things, specifically, repeatedly commanded in the New Testament that we do *not* do in the Church of Christ today. We justify our actions (or lack of same) by saying that the command was given based upon the customs in the 1st Century and that, since the customs have changed, those commands no longer apply to us today or that something else, a modern day equivalent, is substituted in its place.

It is like the "get out of jail free" card in Monopoly, only it is really a "get out of command" card. I have never figured out just how to determine if something was a permanent command or a custom/culture command. They look strikingly similar to me. Continue to read below and see if you agree.

A. Holy Kiss There are five specific times when the New Testament writers told the 1st century Christians to *Greet one another with a holy kiss* (Rom. 16:16; 1 Cor 16:20; 2 Cor. 13:12; 1 Thes. 5:26; 1 Pet. 5:14).

To my knowledge, I have never seen anyone in the Church of Christ greet someone else with a "holy kiss." Instead, we shake hands or hug. We say that it is a matter of custom, that, therefore we do not have to do the actual holy kiss thing.

B. Lift Up Holy Hands 1 Tim. 2:8 says, *I want men everywhere to lift up holy hands in prayer, without anger or disputing.* Would it be acceptable to do this in our assembly Sunday morning?

If someone, in charge of leading a prayer in one of our more conservative churches, decided to ask everyone to lift up their holy hands in prayer, there is a reasonable chance that he would not be asked to lead again. At the very least, some would be uncomfortable, even though it could be justified with scripture.

C. Head Coverings–*Man should uncover his head and woman should cover her head when praying or prophesying.* **1 Cor. 11:2-10 (NIV).**

Is not the requirement for a woman to have her head covered more than just a cultural situation or custom?

v 3 says, . . .*the head of every man is Christ, and the head of every woman is man, and the head of Christ is God.*, then verse 7-10 says, *A man ought not to cover his head since he is the image and glory of God; but the woman is the glory of man. For man did not come from woman, but woman from man; neither was man created for woman, but woman for man. For this reason, ... the woman ought to have a sign of authority on her head.*

Then in verse 16 Paul's determination is apparent when he writes, *If anyone wants to be contentious about this, we have no other practice—nor do the churches of God.*

In spite of the apparently strong reasons for the command, we consider that it is a custom that has changed. We have used the basic principle that, in those days, when a woman took off her head covering, it was a sign of loose morals and sexual promiscuity.

The shaved head indicated that the woman either had been publicly disgraced because of some shameful act or was openly flaunting her independence and her refusal to be in submission to her husband. Having no head covering today does not indicate those things, at least not in the United States; therefore, goes the argument, the requirement no longer applies.

QUESTION: Can we apply and use this basic interpretation everywhere in the New Testament? If not, how do we know when we can use this method of interpretation at all? *How do we know* when it is custom and when it is still binding?

Let us look at the issue of instrumental music in light of this method of interpretation. Keep in mind that our purpose is not to decide whether instrumental music is acceptable or not. If you are concentrating on that, you will miss my point. The purpose is to examine **methods of Bible interpretation,** to see if we are being consistent in our Bible study.

During Old Testament times, instrumental music appeared to be acceptable to God. David often used the instrument in his praises to God (Psa. 92:1-3; 1 Chr. 25:1; Psalms 4; 1 Chr 23:5).

When the Ark of the Covenant was brought back to Jerusalem, David told the leaders of the Levites to appoint their brothers as singers to sing joyful songs, accompanied by musical instruments: lyres, harps and cymbals. (1 Chron. 15:16).

Then, for some reason, when the New Testament was written, the saints were told to *sing psalms, hymns and spiritual songs with gratitude in your hearts to God* (Col 3:16), and in Eph. 5:19 they were told to *speak to one another with psalms, hymns and spiritual songs. Sing and make music in your heart to the Lord.* In these verses there is no direct mention of a mechanical instrument.

Could there have been a cultural reason for this exclusion, one similar to that for women's head coverings? Read what some church historians have said about this:

E.S. Lorenz - Church Music: "Singing, (there was no instrumental accompaniment) was little more than a means of expressing in a practicable, social way, the common faith and experience. . . The music was purely vocal. There was no instrumental accompaniment of any kind... It fell under the ban of the Christian church, as did all other instruments, *because of its pagan association.*"

Alfredo Unterseiner - A Short History of Music: "It was exclusively vocal, for the Christian had an aversion to instruments *which served at pagan feasts.*"

Dr. F.L. Ritter - History of Music From The Christian Era to The Present Time: "Instrumental music was excluded, at first, as having been used by the Rom. at their *depraved festivities; and everything reminding them of heathen worship* could not be endured by the new religionists."

Edward Dickinson - History of Music: ". . .while the *pagan melodies were always sung to an instrumental accompaniment,* the church chant was exclusively vocal."

Is it not the case that just as uncovered heads meant an association with loose morals, instrumental music indicated association with pagan festivals? **If it is acceptable to change the practice of head covering when that association disappeared, would it not also be acceptable to lighten up on our condemnation of those who use instrumental music when it no longer represents pagan feasts? If not, why not?**

And, once again, how do we know what was custom and what is binding? Do we have a consistent method of interpretation? If we assume that the correct method of interpretation is the method we discussed last time ("God Means What He Says"), then the following must be true:

a) Women must wear head coverings (or at least long hair) in the assembly, and

b) We must sing in the worship services without instrumental music.

However, if we assume that the correct method of interpretation has to do with **customs and the culture of the day**, then the following must be true:

a) Women are not required to wear head coverings in today's American culture, and

b) We are not necessarily required to sing without the instrument in our worship services today, since it is no longer primarily associated with pagan feasts.

An objective student of God's Word will not have mixed answers on this. It has got to be one or the other. So, which one is right? Do not answer that just yet. There is more to consider.

Method #3
Examples are Binding

Another method of interpreting the Bible that we often use to "prove" what we want to bind on someone, or to bind on just ourselves as we seek God's instruction, is the method of using examples to determine our course.

Using the Example methodology has to do with the goal of restoring the "pattern" of the 1st century church. It is held that if the first century church did it, then we should do it, even if it was not specifically commanded (unless it had to do with customs and their culture: then we could modify it to meet our current culture).

Conversely, if they did not do it, we should not do it. We should follow their example and do it exactly like they did it. To do it any other way is a sin. Many verses seem, at first glance, to support this interpretation. Consider:

Jn. 13:15 (NIV) *I have set you an example that you should do as I have done for you.*

1 Cor. 10:1-11 (NIV) *For I do not want you to be ignorant of the fact, brothers, that our forefathers were all under the cloud and that they all passed through the sea. They were all baptized into Moses in the cloud and in the sea. They all ate the same spiritual food and drank the same spiritual drink; for they drank from the spiritual rock that accompanied them, and that rock was Christ. Nevertheless, God was not pleased with most of them; their bodies were scattered over the desert. Now these things occurred as examples to keep us from setting our hearts on evil things as they did. Do not be idolaters, as some of them were; as it is written: "The people sat down to eat and drink and got up to indulge in pagan revelry." We should not commit sexual immorality, as some of them did—and in one day twenty-three thousand of them died. We should not test the Lord, as some of them did—and were killed by snakes. And do not grumble, as some of them did—and were killed by the destroying angel. These things happened to them as examples and were written down as warnings for us, on whom the fulfillment of the ages has come.*

1 Cor. 11:1 (NIV) *Follow my example, as I follow the example of Christ.*

Phil. 3:16-17 (NIV) *Only let us live up to what we have already attained. Join with others in following my example, brothers, and take note of those who live according to the pattern we gave you.*

2 Thes. 3:6-9 (NIV) *In the name of the Lord Jesus Christ, we command you, brothers, to keep away from every brother who is idle and does not live according to the teaching you received from us. For you yourselves know how you ought* *to follow our example. We were not idle when we were with you, nor did we eat anyone's food without paying for it. On the contrary, we worked night and day, laboring and toiling so that we would not be a burden to any of you. We did this, not because we do not have the right to such help, but in order to make ourselves a model for you to follow.*

1 Tim. 1:15-16 (NIV) *Here is a trustworthy saying that deserves full acceptance: Christ Jesus came into the world to save sinners–of whom I am the worst. But for that very reason I was shown mercy so that in me, the worst of sinners, Christ Jesus might display his unlimited patience as an example for those who would believe on him and receive eternal life.*

1 Tim. 4:12 (NIV) *Do not let anyone look down on you because you are young, but set an example for the believers in speech, in life, in love, in faith and in purity.*

Tit. 2:7 (NIV) *In everything set them an example by doing what is good. In your teaching show integrity, seriousness*

Heb. 8:5 (NIV) *They serve at a sanctuary that is a copy and shadow of what is in heaven. This is why Moses was warned when he was about to build the tabernacle: "See to it that you make everything according to the pattern shown you on the mountain."*

But, upon a close inspection, it seems that these have little, if any, to do with doctrine or with how the 1st century church worshiped. These examples, that we are to follow, are about how Paul and Christ and others lived their lives. And we should, indeed, follow their examples and live Godly lives.

But when it comes to using this method, I have a few questions, such as, **which part of an example is binding on us today?**

In **Acts 2:43-47 (NIV)** the scriptures tell us, *Everyone was filled with awe, and many wonders and miraculous signs were done by the apostles. All the believers were together and had everything in common. Selling their possessions and goods, they gave to anyone as he had need. Every day they continued to meet together in the temple courts. They broke bread in their homes and ate together with glad and sincere hearts, praising God and enjoying the favor of all the people. And the Lord added to their number daily those who were being saved.*

The example they left us, to sell possessions and goods and to give to every one as they have need and to meet together *every day* in the Temple courts: Is any part of that bound on us today?

When Phillip was going to teach the Ethiopian Eunuch **(Acts 8:27)**, he ran up to the chariot. Is that example binding—about running up to the person I am teaching?

When we look at what the early church did with the money that was collected in the contribution, it was used *only* to help the poor and the needy in the local as well as the other churches.

Also, Paul talked about how he, an evangelist, had the right to receive compensation and how an Elder who worked full time was worthy of "double honor" (honor as in respect and financial support as well).

Yet, we use the contribution for many more things than did the first century church. The congregation of which I am a member even contributes to the local volunteer fire department.

Is not the example of how the early Christians used the church contributions in the first century binding on us today?

It is good for us to consider examples of what the early church and its leaders did. It helps us understand what God wants from us. But, as you can see, we do not use the binding of examples consistently as a method of interpretation because even trying to decide which part of the example we should follow is difficult.

Further, an example implies that there is more than one of something. In other words, an example illustrates one way to execute a principle, but not necessarily the only way.

A Ford is one example of a type of automobile, implying that there is more than one type. Therefore, we cannot use an example as our one correct method of interpretation to determine exclusively what to include or exclude when interpreting God's Word.

It is just an aid. It is just an example, but not necessarily the only example that would be acceptable to God.

Method # 4
Necessary Inference

We have looked at the methods of Bible interpretation involving "God Means What He Says," "Customs and/or Culture" and "Examples are Binding". Another method of interpreting the Bible that we sometimes use to "prove" that what we are doing is right (and to do otherwise would be wrong) is what is termed "Necessary Inference."

A Necessary Inference is something, though neither specifically commanded nor spelled out, is strongly implied by the example. It is similar to an example and often used in conjunction with an example to come to a conclusion.

For instance, in Acts 20:7, Luke starts with, *On the first day of the week we came together to break bread.* There was no specific command to come together on the first day of the week to break bread, here or anywhere else; the verse simply states that they came together on the first day of this particular week to break bread.

In **1 Cor. 16:2 (NIV),** Paul told the Cor., *On the first day of every week, each one of you should set aside a sum of money in keeping with his income, saving it up, so that when I come no collections will have to be made.*

From the coupling of these two passages we may infer that on the first day of every week we are required to partake of the Lord's Supper (Communion, Breaking of the Bread).

With confirmation from non-Christian historians that the early Christians did, in fact eat the Lord's Supper on the first day of each week, we have an example that, combined with a necessary inference, makes it a requirement that we also eat the Supper on the first day of every week.

Some say that if you do not take Communion on the first day of every week, you are in danger of losing your soul to the devil; that it would, in fact, be sinful to take it on any other day of the week (even if you took it on Sunday as well).

A few weeks ago, a brother, when talking about clapping, said, "If God desired the clapping of hands, do not we believe that He would have stated so in no uncertain terms?" This brother does not make that same statement when talking about taking the Lord's Supper on the first day of every week.

So I ask now, "If God desired the taking of the Lord's Supper on the first day of every week, do not we believe that he would have stated so in no uncertain terms?" Would it not have been such a simple and easy and clarifying thing for him to say, "On the first day of every week, come together to break the bread?"

But God, in his wisdom, chose not to. So we, in our wisdom, by using "necessary inference," have made it a requirement by which we are willing to condemn those who do not do it.

I take the Lord's Supper on the first day of every week. I think it is a good thing to do. But to make it a requirement based upon what the Bible reveals to us requires that we put much emphasis on a speculative method of interpretation; and, that we are treading on dangerous ground when we condemn others who take it less often or on other days in addition to or instead of the first day of the week. We just do not have the scriptural grounds to do so.

Also, we are selective about when we use Necessary Inference. We do not use it when studying 1 Cor 11 in which Paul talks about how women should not pray or prophesy with their heads uncovered. Would not the necessary inference be that it is acceptable for women to pray or prophecy with their heads covered?

[Another question: Was Paul talking about the need for women to wear these head coverings only in the assembly, or anytime they were in public? How do you know?]

In **1 Tim 3:11** when Paul speaks about the qualifications for a deaconess, does not that imply that there should be the office of a deaconess in the church? Some say he is talking about deacon's wives, but why would Paul talk about the qualifications of deacon's wives when he does not talk about the qualifications of Elder's wives?

Method #5

Speak Where the Bible Speaks

One of the foundational elements which the Church of Christ has used to determine "sound doctrine" is that, when it comes to interpreting scripture, we should "speak where the Bible speaks and be silent where the Bible is silent."

(**Note:** I have not seen where the Bible commands this doctrine. I have seen the one about not adding or taking away from the prophecy, but nothing about speaking where Bible speaks, and silence where Bible is silent. On that basis, is it not therefore a violation of its own principle?)

In other words, for the first half of the quotation, if something is commanded in the Bible, we should obey it, because that is what the Bible teaches. That is very straight-forward and a simple (not easy, but simple) method of determining what the Bible teaches.

However, the second half of the quotation sounds just as straight-forward—but gets murky when you start trying to apply it. The rub comes when you are trying to decide whether the silence of the scriptures on a particular subject means it is forbidden, since it is not authorized (this is the more traditional interpretation), or whether that silence indicates it is permitted since it is not forbidden. Some of my brothers use it both ways, depending on the subject.

I've never seen the following statements, which were made by Paul, included in the discussion on this topic. They would seem to lean toward freedom:

> **1 Cor. 6:12 (NIV)** *"Everything is permissible for me"—but not everything is beneficial. "Everything is permissible for me"—but I will not be mastered by anything.*

> **1 Cor. 10:23 (NIV)** *"Everything is permissible"--but not everything is beneficial. "Everything is permissible"--but not everything is constructive.*

What I have seen are the following discussions. It is said, on the one hand, that it is wrong to sing a song while the congregation is taking the Lord's Supper, because there is neither example nor command specifically authorizing it. The same thing is true about clapping during worship. We are authorized to sing and to pray and to preach, but we are never specifically authorized to clap—so it is forbidden. Other things not specifically authorized are choirs (during the worship services), praise teams and instruments of music.

On the other hand, since the Bible does not specifically forbid Sunday School Bible Classes, it is permissible to have them. The same is true of having youth ministers. It is not forbidden, therefore it is allowed. It does not specifically forbid the use of the term "worship service" so it is permissible to use it (even though it is never used in the Bible). And the list goes on and is different for each person.

The reality is that it is impossible, with any degree of accuracy or credibility, to use this statement to determine what God wants.

Method # 6

A Better Way

Recently, my wife and I traveled a few hours north to attend a wedding of a friend. As we often do, we took the back roads to see more of the scenery.

As we came through a little town having a population of 575, I noticed a Church of Christ sign in front of a little white brick building on the left.

We turned at the town's intersection and drove a few blocks to where I saw another Church of Christ sign in front of a little red brick building. This building did not have any rooms outside the main building, so we decided it must be the "anti-Sunday school" church in town.

Seeing these two churches made me think of the similarity that this town had with every other small town in the state of Texas: Most, if not all, have at least two Churches of Christ. We have three in our small town—and that is not because we are growing. In short, it is because of the way we have chosen to interpret scripture.

Previously, by using one of our methods of interpretation, I proved, using book, chapter and verse, that we must greet one another with a holy kiss, and that no other greeting is authorized or acceptable.

That same method of interpretation is what we have traditionally used to prove that we are authorized, and even commanded, to sing, *only*, and therefore, that we are not allowed to clap, use an instrument or any other "noise maker" in our worship—that to do so would be sinful.

My goal in writing this holy kiss example and in comparing it with our singing, only, example, was to illustrate how one's conclusions on any topic can be altered by simply choosing a different method of interpretation than has been traditionally applied.

When the leadership of one church selects a different method for drawing conclusions on a topic than does the leadership of the church down the road, different doctrinal conclusions are inevitable.

If, then, the leadership of that one church makes it a policy that they will only fellowship with churches who are in agreement on doctrinal issues, division and continued separation is unavoidable, which leads to multiple Churches of Christ in every town.

(As an aside, it is the nature of the more liberal churches to accept the more conservative churches and to esteem them as brothers. It is the nature of more conservative churches to reject the more liberal churches due to the fact that accepting more liberal churches would be seen as the equivalent of condoning error and promoting false teaching.)

To resolve these separation problems, we need to figure out a way to agree with one another in regard to interpreting God's Word.

The solution to this problem lies in finding a single method of interpretation that can be reasonably applied to every issue. **Any method of interpretation (including the methods we have discussed in the previous chapters), that cannot be applied to every issue, is divisive by nature, and therefore should be rejected.**

In the place of those rejected methods, we should begin applying the one method that will work for all topics, namely, the method of looking for the principles being taught.

It is the principle that counts.

The key to understanding God's will is in finding **the principles being taught** by God's Word. I do not have a problem with getting out the microscope to see what the command or custom or example or the necessary inference was as long as we do not stop there.

We need to also back up and look at the purpose of the command or example; What is the principle being taught in each situation? **The principle being taught is the most important thing.**

Customs and the meanings of words and implications of various situations are constantly changing, but the principles that God is teaching will never change.

Even the commands that God gave were specific to a time and had a purpose for that time. When looking at the purpose of a command or the principle involved in that command, it might be seen to have a different application today (for examples, "Greet one another with a holy kiss." "Women should wear a head covering").

A command is not as important as the principle being taught. In this case (greetings and head coverings), we should bond with one another and show respect to God and to one another. And that is what we should be looking for, the principles being taught, to apply to our lives.

When asked what was the greatest command, Jesus gave a two-for-one answer; that the greatest command was to love God and love one's fellow man. This duel command embodies the principle that it is teaching.

Not only does the command embody the principle, it also sheds light on how far-reaching is this principle. And, it is stated in various ways, several times in the New Testament.

Matt. 22:37-40 (NIV) *Jesus replied: 'Love the Lord your God with all your heart and with all your soul and with all your mind. This is the first and greatest commandment. And the second is like it: 'Love your neighbor as yourself.* **All the law and the prophets hang on these two commandments.'**

Rom. 13:8-10 (NIV) *Let no debt remain outstanding, except the continuing debt to love one another, for he who loves his fellowman* **has fulfilled the law.** *The commandments, "Do not commit adultery," "Do not murder," "Do not steal," "Do not covet," and whatever other commandment there may be, are summed up in this one rule: "Love your neighbor as yourself."* **Love does no harm to its neighbor. Therefore love is the fulfillment of the law.**

Matt. 7:12 (NIV) *So in everything, do to others what you would have them do to you, for **this sums up the Law and the Prophets.***

Gal. 5:13,14 (NIV) *You, my brothers, were called to be free. But do not use your freedom to indulge the sinful nature; rather, serve one another in love. **The entire law is summed up in a single command: "Love your neighbor as yourself.***

Gal. 6:2 (NIV) *Carry each other's burdens, and **in this way you will fulfill the law of Christ.***

Each of these passages concludes with an indication that all of God's laws can be summed up by and/or are fulfilled by doing those two things—loving God and loving your neighbor.

The Romans passage even tells why it is the fulfillment of the law—because it does no harm to its neighbor. If you truly love your neighbor, you will not be killing them or coveting or committing adultery. Therefore, love sums up the principles embodied in the law.

In **Mk. 7:9-13 (NIV)**, Jesus dealt with some Pharisees and Scribes who were using scripture selectively in an attempt to cancel the principles that God was teaching. Specifically, they were using a command from God stating that any vow made to God could not be violated (Numbers 30:2) as an excuse to cancel the command from God to "Honor thy father and mother."

In the real life application, when the parents of these Pharisees (or their followers) needed financial help, the Pharisees would tell them that the money ordinarily set aside to help the parents had already been vowed to God, therefore, it couldn't be used to help the parents.

Jesus told them, *You have a fine way of setting aside the commands of God in order to observe your own traditions! For Moses said, 'Honor your father and your mother,' and, 'Anyone who curses his father or mother must be put to death.' But you say that if a man says to his father or mother: 'Whatever help you might otherwise have received from me is Corban' (that is, a gift devoted to God), then you no longer let him do anything for his father or mother. Thus you nullify the Word of God by your tradition that you have handed down. And you do many things like that."*

This is an example of using selective interpretation to void the principle that God intended—that love does no harm to its neighbor (or parents, in this case). If we are not careful, we can violate the principle that God is teaching, by interpreting scripture in a way that does harm to our neighbor—such as condemning someone for something that God does not condemn.

When we do this, we have misinterpreted the scripture, because we have violated the Godly principle.

In the gospels, Jesus illustrated how people had failed to achieve God's purposes, by interpreting scripture in a legalistic manner, and applying a very literal letter to the law without regard to the principle or spirit of that law. And He scolded them for it.

The passage below describes how a woman came and performed an act of worship which was neither specifically commanded nor authorized. Can you imagine—an unauthorized act of worship? **How would Jesus respond to this unauthorized act of worship?** Observers, legalistic in their interpretation-method, were upset, because she did not follow the authorized list.

Jesus, whose list was apparently more focused on the principle of loving him and worshiping him, did not get upset with her at all—quite the contrary.

Mk. 14:3-8 (NIV) *While he was in Bethany, reclining at the table in the home of a man known as Simon the Leper, a woman came with an alabaster jar of very expensive perfume, made of pure nard. She broke the jar and poured the perfume on his head. Some of those present were saying indignantly to one another, "Why this waste of perfume? It could have been sold for more than a year's wages and the money given to the poor." And they rebuked her harshly. "Leave her alone," said Jesus. "Why are you bothering her? She has done a beautiful thing to me. The poor you will always have with you, and you can help them any time you want. But you will not always have me. She did what she could. She poured perfume on my body beforehand to prepare for my burial.*

Today, because of our use of the "command" method of interpretation, the legalistic obedience to a specific and exclusive list of actions seems to take precedence over the principle that God wants from our heart.

He wants our worship to be an outpouring of that heart. If he has our hearts and our hearts are bursting with the desire to express our love to him, he does not seem to be as concerned about our method of expressing that love as he is with the fact that we want to express it.

Some of my brothers and sisters, on the other hand, want to squelch this unauthorized behavior since it is not specifically authorized in scripture. That is too bad.

There are many more examples which I will not delve deeply into now for the sake of time and space. But if you study passages like Matt. 12:1-14 (and Mark 2:23-3:6, its companion) in which Jesus and his disciples picked grain on the Sabbath and are criticized for it, you will see that Jesus talks about David eating the showbread, which was unlawful, and that the "Sabbath is made for man, not man for the Sabbath."

He also told them that if they *had known what these words mean, 'I desire mercy, not sacrifice,' you would not have condemned the innocent.* In all of these cases he is pointing to the need to look for the principles that God is teaching and not to a legalistic faultfinding. He expresses the exact same concept in Micah 6:6-8 in which he offers a principle-ladened summary,

> **Mic. 6:6-8 (NIV)** *With what shall I come before the Lord and bow down before the exalted God? Shall I come before him with burnt offerings, with calves a year old? Will the Lord be pleased with thousands of rams, with ten thousand rivers of oil? Shall I offer my firstborn for my transgression, the fruit of my body for the sin of my soul? He has showed you, O man, what is good.* **And what does the Lord require of you? To act justly and to love mercy and to walk humbly with your God.**

To correctly divide the word of truth, our primary focus, perhaps our *only* focus, *must* be on the **principles** that God is teaching. That is the only way in which the Bible can make sense and be consistently understood in every culture, every country, and every century.

To find and apply Godly principles is key to clearing away so much of the religious clutter and garbage that entangles us in bitter disputes and divisions and doubts. It is the better way. It leads us to Godly answers.

God bless you as you consider these thoughts.

Regulations for Worship

God gave (what amounts to) ninety-two pages of rules and regulations in the Old Testament. These included instructions on how to worship and how to live, including something as specific as what to do if you came across a bird's nest beside the road.

In the New Testament God chose not to give us a book, or even a chapter, which spells out the regulations for how we should conduct our "Worship Services" today.

Man, being man, decided that he needed to create his own list of regulations for worship for the New Testament church. Then, using that newly created list of regulations, he began binding it on himself and others. This was not what God intended, according to scripture, but it is what man does.

Consider the following:

Old Testament Regulations for Worship

In the Old Testament, God went into great detail about how his children should worship him. He was very specific about where to worship, how to worship, the dimensions and details of the worship facility, when to have a religious feast, what specific things to do at that feast and in fact he had a whole host of commands and regulations—very specific and detailed commands and regulations.

I went through my Bible a while back and compiled all of these detailed commands and regulations into one document. The document wound up being ninety-two pages long.

Ninety-two pages of detailed regulations. It was very clear what God wanted and what God meant.

Here is an interesting sample of those regulations. You may be surprised about how detailed God got in some areas. He even told what to do if one came across a bird's nest beside the road and how to build the roof on a house. He left nothing to chance.

Ex. 21:16-19 (NIV) *Anyone who kidnaps another and either sells him or still has him when he is caught must be put to death. Anyone who curses his father or mother must be put to death. If men quarrel and one hits the other with a stone or with his fist and he does not die but is confined to bed, the one who struck the blow will not be held responsible if the other gets up and walks around outside with his staff; however, he must pay the injured man for the loss of his time and see that he is completely healed.*

Ex. 26:30-35 (NIV) *Set up the tabernacle according to the plan shown you on the mountain. Make a curtain of blue, purple and scarlet yarn and finely twisted linen, with cherubim worked into it by a skilled craftsman. Hang it with gold hooks on four posts of acacia wood overlaid with gold and standing on four silver bases. Hang the curtain from the clasps and place the ark of the Testimony behind the curtain. The curtain will separate the Holy Place from the Most Holy Place. Put the atonement cover on the ark of the Testimony in the Most Holy Place. Place the table outside the curtain on the north side of the tabernacle and put the lamp stand opposite it on the south side.*

Lev. 11:29-31 (NIV) *Of the animals that move about on the ground, these are unclean for you: the weasel, the rat, any kind of great lizard, the gecko, the monitor lizard, the wall lizard, the skink and the chameleon. Of all those that move along the ground, these are unclean for you. Whoever touches them when they are dead will be unclean till evening.*

Deut 22:1-12 (NIV) *If you see your brother's ox or sheep straying, do not ignore it but be sure to take it back* *to him. If the brother does not live near you or if you do not know who he is, take it home with you and keep it until he comes looking for it. Then give it back to him. Do the same if you find your brother's donkey or his cloak or anything he loses. Do not ignore it. If you see your brother's donkey or his ox fallen on the road, do not ignore it. Help him get it to its feet. A woman must not wear men's clothing, nor a man wear women's clothing, for the Lord your God detests anyone who does this. If you come across a bird's nest beside the road, either in a tree or on the ground, and the mother is sitting on the young or on the eggs, do not take the mother with the young. You may take the young, but be sure to let the mother go, so that it may go well with you and you may have a long life.*

When you build a new house, make a parapet around your roof so that you may not bring the guilt of bloodshed on your house if someone falls from the roof.

Do not plant two kinds of seed in your vineyard; if you do, not only the crops you plant but also the fruit of the vineyard will be defiled.

Do not plow with an ox and a donkey yoked together. Do not wear clothes of wool and linen woven together. Make tassels on the four corners of the cloak you wear.

There is no doubt about what he wanted them to do. Or is there? Through the years, the Pharisees would have great discussions about how to uphold various phases of the law.

Regarding the Sabbath Regulations the Pharisees had debates over various matters—*could a man wear a wooden leg on the Sabbath? Was it lawful to eat an egg laid on the Sabbath? Some knots could be tied or untied on the Sabbath, but not others. Vinegar, if swallowed, could be used to relieve a sore throat, but it could not be gargled. No woman was to look in a mirror on the Sabbath lest, seeing a gray hair, she might be tempted to pull it out.* [2]

The reality was and is that no one was able to keep the Law perfectly, except Jesus Christ.

Did the children of Israel obey the Law?

No! Why not?

> **Rom. 9:31 (NIV)** *but Israel, who pursued a law of righteousness, has not attained it.*

> **Rom. 3:23 (NIV)** *for all have sinned and fall short of the glory of God,*

> **Jas. 2:10 (NIV)** *For whoever keeps the whole law and yet stumbles at just one point is guilty of breaking all of it.*

They did not keep the law and neither can we. And that was part of the purpose of the law—to lead us to Christ.

> **Gal. 3:24 [KJV]** *So the law was put in charge to lead us to Christ that we might be justified by faith. Wherefore the law was our schoolmaster to bring us unto Christ, that we might be justified by faith.*

It did that by making us conscious of sin.

> **Rom. 3:19-20 (NIV)** *Now we know that whatever the law says, it says to those who are under the law, so that every mouth may be silenced and the whole world held accountable to God. Therefore no one will be declared righteous in his sight by observing the law; rather, through the law we become conscious of sin.*

So what did God do with it?

He set it aside.

> **Heb. 7:18-19 (NIV)** *The former regulation is set aside because it was weak and useless (for the law made nothing perfect), and a better hope is introduced, by which we draw near to God.*

Why would God give us a law that was impossible to obey?

Because he wanted us to come to the realization that we can not do it alone.

> **Rom. 3:27-28 (NIV)** *Where, then, is boasting? It is excluded. On what principle? On that of observing the law? No, but on that of faith. For we maintain that a man is justified by faith apart from observing the law.*

> **Gal. 2:16 (NIV)** *know that a man is not justified by observing the law, but by faith in Jesus Christ. So we, too, have put our faith in Christ Jesus that we may be justified by faith in Christ and not by observing the law, because by observing the law no one will be justified.*

New Testament Regulations for Worship

As we turn to the New Testament, God did *not* give us a book or even a chapter regarding the regulations for worship. He left it out.

Why do you think he did that? Do you think that was by **accident**? Do you think God might have **forgotten** to include a detailed list of worship regulations?

Since God did not give us the detailed commandments and regulations in the NT, some of our well-meaning brothers decided that we should worship according to "the 1st century pattern," that we should see what they did back then and do it ourselves today. So they scoured the New Testament and used commands, examples and necessary inferences and made a new list of worship regulations.

As time went on, they decided that if we do not follow this specific list of new regulations, then God is going to send us to Hell.

For decades, if not centuries, we have condemned others based upon what we considered to be their lack of compliance to what amounts to manmade regulations for New Testament Worship.

Note that **most, if not all, of those regulations have to do with how technically correct one worships God during that official weekly assembly time on Sunday.** We have said "You cannot be a member of the one true church unless you follow this pattern."

My question is, "if God chose **not** to give us external regulations for worship, why should we create them ourselves and bind them on ourselves and others?" Does it not make sense that if God wanted to bind us to the 1st Century pattern that he would have given us a specific list of worship regulations, as he did in the Old Testament?

The truth is that we human beings, like to have a specific checklist that we can rely on. But God does not want us relying on a check list. He does not want us relying on external regulations. And that is what we have a tendency to do—rely on following a checklist so we can feel sure that we qualify because we have followed all the rules. Consider the following.

Heb. 9:1-2, 10 (NIV) *Now the first covenant had regulations for worship and also an earthly sanctuary. A tabernacle was set up. In its first room were the lamp stand . . . They are only a matter of food and drink and various ceremonial washings—external regulations **applying until the time of the new order**.*

The new order is here. External regulations do not apply any more as a matter of salvation.

Instead, God, who gave us ninety-two pages of external regulations in the Old Testament and who emphasized them repeatedly has now, in the New Testament, done everything he can to de-emphasize external worship regulations.

> **Jn. 4:21-24 (NIV)** *Jesus declared, Believe me, woman, a time is coming when you will worship the Father neither on this mountain nor in Jerusalem. You Samaritans worship what you do not know; we worship what we do know, for salvation is from the Jews. Yet a time is coming and has now come when the* **true worshipers will worship the Father in spirit and truth**, *for they are the kind of worshipers the Father seeks. God is spirit, and his worshipers must worship in* **spirit and in truth**.

This passage describes a critical event in the life of Christ's followers—a change in regard to our worship of God. Until that moment, worship had to do with a **time** and a **place** and a **ritual**. After that moment, it no longer had to do with those things.

The *true* worshipers, from that point forward, must worship in spirit and truth. What does that mean?

The **truth** part has to do with a genuineness of heart, sincerity and a desire to be what God wants us to be. Our worship to God must rise up from deep within us.

We can see what the **spiritual** part of that equation is by taking a look at Romans 12. Note the following:

> **Rom. 12:1 (NIV)** *Therefore, I urge you, brothers, in view of God's mercy, to* ***offer your bodies as living***

sacrifices, *holy and pleasing to God—**this is your spiritual act of worship**.*

From that point on, including today, our spiritual act of worship is not supposed to be about what we do for an hour on Sunday morning. It is about how we offer our bodies as living sacrifices—how we live our lives—all day, every day.

Paul then spends the rest of Romans twelve explaining what that looks like in real life—this spiritual act of worship.

Rom. 12:2-21 (NIV) *Do not conform any longer to the pattern of this world, but be transformed by the renewing of your mind. Then you will be able to test and approve what God's will is—his good, pleasing and perfect will. For by the grace given me I say to every one of you: Do not think of yourself more highly than you ought, but rather think of yourself with sober judgment, in accordance with the measure of faith God has given you.*

Just as each of us has one body with many members, and these members do not all have the same function, so in Christ we who are many form one body, and each member belongs to all the others. We have different gifts, according to the grace given us. If a man's gift is prophesying, let him use it in proportion to his faith.

If it is serving, let him serve; if it is teaching, let him teach; if it is encouraging, let him encourage; if it is contributing to the needs of others, let him give generously; if it is leadership, let him govern diligently; if it is showing mercy, let him do it cheerfully.

Love must be sincere. Hate what is evil; cling to what is good. Be devoted to one another in brotherly love. Honor one another above yourselves. Never be lacking in zeal, but keep your spiritual fervor, serving the Lord. Be joyful in hope, patient in affliction, faithful in prayer.

Share with God's people who are in need. Practice hospitality. Bless those who persecute you; bless and do not curse. Rejoice with those who rejoice; mourn with those who mourn. Live in harmony with one another. Do not be proud, but be willing to associate with people of low position. Do not be conceited.

Do not repay anyone evil for evil. Be careful to do what is right in the eyes of everybody. If it is possible, as far as it depends on you, live at peace with everyone. Do not take revenge, my friends, but leave room for God's wrath, for it is written: It is mine to avenge; I will repay, says the Lord.

On the contrary: If your enemy is hungry, feed him; if he is thirsty, give him something to drink. In doing this, you will heap burning coals on his head. Do not be overcome by evil, but overcome evil with good.

Paul carries on throughout the next few chapters talking about how Christians, who are offering their bodies as living sacrifices, live their lives.

Godly worship is about all day every day, not solely for that one hour on Sunday that we have focused on so much in our efforts to be pure.

When I see passages like **Matt. 25:31-36 (NIV)** and the focus on salvation issues in that passage as compared to the typical salvation issues that I have heard preached from the pulpit for so many years, I just cannot help but think, "How are we missing this?" Notice in this passage, the criteria that the Lord uses for separating the sheep and the goats.;

Matt. 25:31-36 (NIV) *When the Son of Man comes in his glory, and all the angels with him, he will sit on his throne in heavenly glory. All the nations will be gathered before him, and he will separate the people one from another as a shepherd separates the sheep from the goats. He will put the sheep on his right and the goats on his left. Then the King will say to those on his right, 'Come, you who are blessed by my Father; take your inheritance, the kingdom prepared for you since the creation of the world. For I was hungry and you gave me something to eat, I was thirsty and you gave me something to drink, I was a stranger and you invited me in, I needed clothes and you clothed me, I was sick and you looked after me, I was in prison and you came to visit me.'*

Do you think that maybe we have been focusing on the wrong things from our pulpits and in our Bible classes?

Reflect on the following:

Rom. 8:1-2 (NIV) *Therefore, there is now no condemnation for those who are in Christ Jesus, because through Christ Jesus the law of the Spirit of life set me free from the law of sin and death.*

2 Cor. 3:6 (NIV) *He has made us competent as ministers of a new covenant—not of the letter but of the Spirit; for the letter kills, but the Spirit gives life.*

Once again, God, who gave us all these external regulations in the Old Testament and who emphasized them repeatedly has now, in the New Testament, done everything he can to de-emphasize external worship regulations.

God does not want us relying on a list of rules and regulations. He wants us to rely on him.

Gal. 2:16 (NIV) *know that a man is not justified by observing the law, but by faith in Jesus Christ. So we, too, have put our faith in Christ Jesus that we may be justified by faith in Christ and not by observing the law, because by observing the law no one will be justified.*

He has set us free from those regulations. And in fact, he warns us in Galatians 5 that if we try to be justified by following the regulations, that we have fallen away from grace.

Gal. 5:1-6 (NIV) *It is for freedom that Christ has set us free. Stand firm, then, and do not let yourselves be burdened again by a yoke of slavery. Mark my words! I, Paul, tell you that if you let yourselves be circumcised, Christ will be of no value to you at all. Again I declare to every man who lets himself be circumcised that he is obligated to obey the whole law.* **You who are trying to be justified by law have been alienated from Christ; you have fallen away from grace**. *But by faith we eagerly await through the Spirit the righteousness for which we hope. For in Christ Jesus neither circumcision nor uncircumcision has any value.** **The only thing that counts is faith expressing itself through love.**

What God wants from New Testament Christians is faith expressing itself through love. Let us free ourselves from the bondage of relying on our regulations for worship.

God's will for us is not about the Sunday morning worship rules and regulations. It is about the heart and living the Godly life every day of the week.

*Some of the Jewish Christians were trying to force Gentiles to follow the Jewish regulations about being circumcised before they would accept them as Christian brothers. This was not what God wanted. Circumcision was no longer required when the New covenant took effect.

Rule Keeping Worship

There is a passage that is amazing when we consider what it says. It talks about rule keeping worship and how the mentality behind such worship pulls us back to the basic principles of this world rather than to righteous and Godly living.

I will reveal to you where it is found in a moment. But first, I ask you to read it and then fill in the blanks at the very end. You will see that whatever goes into those three blanks is key to understanding the purpose of our worship. The passage says:

Since you died with Christ to the basic principles of this world, why, as though you still belonged to it, do you submit to its rules: "Do not handle! Do not taste! Do not touch!"? These are all destined to perish with use, because they are based on human commands and teachings. Such regulations indeed have an appearance of wisdom, with their self-imposed worship, their false humility and their harsh treatment of the body, but they lack any value in _____ _____ _____.

Do you get the sense that those final words are going to indicate something of value that our worship service is supposed to bring?

Can you see that this passage indicates that our worship is not about following a list of regulations for worship and rule keeping, but that it is about something more than that?

I ask you to read the passage one more time and to guess what the three words are saying. What is the logical answer? Then I will tell you the three words.

The passage is Col. 2:20-23 (NIV). The three missing words are "restraining sensual indulgence." What?

Are we supposed to leave our worship, having been influenced to have a greater, heart-felt desire to restrain our sensual indulgence? Is that what God wants?

Or, are we supposed to leave worship feeling good about having kept all the sound doctrinal rules for worship?

Are we, worshiping God, supposed to be inspired to live Godly lives and love our fellow man and be more dedicated to God and his Word because of something that happens when we come together to worship?

Or, are we supposed to feel gratified because we have pointed out all the error being taught in the other churches around town?

Our worship should not be about leaving with the focus being, "It was a good service because no rules were violated today." That is not the key ingredient that God is looking for, nor does it bring to us what he wants to give us.

Rule-keeping does not bring joy. Rule-keeping does not inspire. Rule-keeping does not bring that peace that "passeth all understanding" (Phil 4:7 KJV)—because it is not a heart-activity; Instead, it is a checklist-activity that removes the feeling of guilt for a little while—and it totally misses the point.

Godly worship recharges our spiritual batteries; focuses our hearts on being grateful for the grace and mercy that God has bestowed upon us; and inspires us to reach out to the lost and to let our *light so shine that others may see our good works and give glory to our father who is in heaven* (Matt. 5:16).

I encourage each of us to notice what thought-patterns cross our minds during and after the worship assembly. Do we focus on whether or not we have kept the rules, or on praising God and looking for ways to be more like him. How we answer that question will go a long way in revealing whether or not we have got his message right.

K.I.S.S.
(Keep It Simple Smartie)

In my earlier days I would dig deep into the Word to find God's hidden truths. I got out my magnifying glass, microscope, telescope, binoculars, monocle, reading glasses pick and shovel and any other tool I could think of to dig in to and expose the tiniest spots in the Word of God. I wanted to be able to dissect it to the core so that I could understand exactly what he had in mind.

Over the past few years I have come to realize that, though there are some benefits to digging that deep, the reality is you do not have to be a scholar to see the big picture. God reveals it over and over with his very simple messages which are scattered throughout the Bible.

And sometimes, its simplicity is surprising. I have compiled some of these simple messages to illustrate what I mean.

A.) In Luke 10, Jesus was approached by a lawyer—an expert in the law—who tested him with the question, "Teacher, what must I do to inherit eternal life?" Jesus answered the question with a question (two questions, actually). "What is written in the law? How do you read it?"

He responded with what Jesus called "the correct answer:" Love God and love your neighbor as yourself: *"Do this and you will live."* Then, attempting to justify himself, the lawyer asked who is his neighbor, which question led Jesus to tell the Parable of the Good Samaritan. Then, Jesus told the expert in the law to "go and do likewise" (i.e.:, to show mercy and compassion).

Think about Jesus' answer. Is this instruction just a little too simplistic when one wants to know how to inherit eternal life? Shouldn't there be more information about obeying Godly worship regulations?

~~~~~

B.) Acts 15 presents an interesting passage. Some men had come down from Judea to Antioch and were teaching that the people could not be saved unless they were circumcised.

After much debate, Paul and Barnabas and some other believers were appointed to go up to Jerusalem to meet with the apostles and elders about this question.

The final outcome of the council—the conclusion reached by these men—was in a letter saying they are not going to burden the believers with anything beyond the following: *You are to abstain from food sacrificed to idols, from blood, from the meat of strangled animals and from sexual immorality.*

What? That is it? That is what came out of a group of men going all the way to Jerusalem and convening with the apostles and elders and having a big giant discussion about circumcision?

The last line of the letter is, *You will do well to avoid these things.* Shouldn't there have been more to it than that?

Part of what is interesting about this letter is that, later, in 1 Cor. 8:4, we find out that in reality there is nothing wrong with eating food offered to idols, unless, by doing so, you cause a weak brother to stumble. And yet, it made the list of four items to be included in the letter to the churches. Interesting, nothing about rules of worship.

~~~~~

C.) In Gal. 2, Paul told the churches about his conversion and subsequent activities and about how he had been appointed to go to the Gentiles, and how James and Peter and John had agreed to it.

He then said: *All they asked was that we should continue to remember the poor, the very thing I was eager to do.*

What an unexpected thing for them to ask. Why would they say that? Why did they not remind him to make sure everyone carried out proper worship regulations? Did they think Paul might stop remembering the poor because he was ministering to the Gentiles?

Was remembering the poor more important than how they worshiped? Or was it so important to minister to the poor that they did not want to leave any doubt as to *its* importance? It is something to think about—this thing they wanted him to remember to do.

D.) In Matthew (as we have already talked about) we read about how Jesus, when he comes in his glory, will separate the people from one another as a shepherd separates the sheep from the goats.

Matt. 25:34-36 (NIV) *Then the King will say to those on his right, 'Come, you who are blessed by my Father; take your inheritance, the kingdom prepared for you since the creation of the world. For I was hungry and you gave me something to eat, I was thirsty and you gave me something to drink, I was a stranger and you invited me in, I needed clothes and you clothed me, I was sick and you looked after me, I was in prison and you came to visit me.'*

Is that the scriptural way to judge who goes to heaven and who does not. Is there a lesson in that passage for us?

~~~~~

E.) The book of James has a description in it of what God considers to be pure and faultless religion. Take a look.

Jas. 1:27 (NIV) *Religion that God our Father accepts as **pure and faultless** is this: to look after orphans and widows in their distress and to keep oneself from being polluted by the world.*

That is pure and faultless religion? What about all the important things—you know, the worship time things?

~~~~~

F.) What is the one thing that we must do above all— and why should we do it?

1 Pet. 4:8 (NIV) *8 Above all, love each other deeply,*

*because **love covers over a multitude of sins.***

What kinds of sins do you think love covers? Could it cover the types of things that we have used to mercilessly condemn people?

~~~~~

G.) One of my favorite verses in the Bible is **Mic. 6:6-8 (NIV)**

*With what shall I come before the Lord and bow down before the exalted God? Shall I come before him with burnt offerings, with calves a year old? Will the Lord be pleased with thousands of rams, with ten thousand rivers of oil? Shall I offer my firstborn for my transgression, the fruit of my body for the sin of my soul? He has showed you, O man, what is good. **And what does the Lord require of you? To act justly and to love mercy and to walk humbly with your God.***

~~~~~

H.) According to the Bible, what is the only thing that counts?

Gal. 5:6 (NIV) *6 For in Christ Jesus neither circumcision nor uncircumcision has any value.* **The only thing that counts** *is faith expressing itself through love.*

~~~~~

I.) The following is a great summary statement that should put some things in perspective for us:

Hos. 6:6 (NIV) *For I desire mercy, not sacrifice, and acknowledgment of God rather than burnt offerings.*

J.) How would you sum up the entire law?

Gal. 5:13-14 (NIV) *You, my brothers, were called to be free. But do not use your freedom to indulge the sinful nature; rather, serve one another in love. The* **entire law is summed up in a single command:** *"Love your neighbor as yourself."*

There are four additional passages that confirm something similar to what you've just read from Galations. We mentioned them earlier, but they are important enough to mention again. They are as follows:

Matt. 22:37-40 (NIV) *Jesus replied: 'Love the Lord your God with all your heart and with all your soul and with all your mind. This is the first and greatest commandment. And the second is like it: 'Love your neighbor as yourself.* **All the law and the prophets hang on these two commandments.'**

Rom. 13:8-10 (NIV) *Let no debt remain outstanding, except the continuing debt to love one another, for he who loves his fellowman* **has fulfilled the law.** *The commandments, "Do not commit adultery," "Do not murder," "Do not steal," "Do not covet," and whatever other commandment there may be, are summed up in this one rule: "Love your neighbor as yourself."* **Love does no harm to its neighbor. Therefore love is the fulfillment of the law.**

Matt. 7:12 (NIV) *"So in everything, do to others what you would have them do to you, for* **this sums up the Law and the Prophets.**

Gal. 6:2 (NIV) *Carry each other's burdens, and* **in this way you will fulfill the law of Christ.**

Each of these passages is concluded with a statement that indicates that all of God's laws can be summed up and/or are fulfilled by doing these two things—**loving God** and **loving your neighbor.**

The Romans passage even tells why it is the fulfillment of the law—because it does no harm to its neighbor. If you truly love your neighbor you will not be killing them or coveting or committing adultery with them. Therefore, love sums up the principles embodied in the law.

Though we have had a tendency to make our lives very complicated with all kinds of religious rules and regulations, it seems that God's simple message, about loving him and loving others, was the one he was trying to get across to his children. As the verses above will attest, God's truths are simple and profound.

Instead of just taking them as he gave them, it seems that, to some degree, the rules themselves have become our God. We have replaced God with regulations for worship. We have basically said that the people who do not follow these certain specific regulations for worship cannot go to heaven. I am convinced that we have overshot the mark.

What would it be like if we all worried less about the regulations and condemning those who disagreed with us about those regulations, and instead we just made it our earnest aim to love God and love our fellow man?

The 80/20 Rule

There is a commonly known rule that is called the 80/20 rule (*The Pareto Principle*), which states that many things in life are divided into 80/20 ratios. For example, in most situations, eighty percent of the people do twenty percent of the work (and twenty percent of the people do eighty percent of the work). Eighty percent of the business profits come from twenty percent of the customers. The principle can be carried over into many other parts of our lives.

It is my conviction that, for most of my life in the Church of Christ, eighty percent of our discussions and sermons and focus was dedicated to determining and enforcing the biblically-acceptable worship regulations (for the one-to-three hours per week that we are assembled), and twenty percent of our time and efforts were dedicated to the discussion about how to live Godly lives and other things.

When I read the New Testament, it seems to be just the opposite. Eighty percent is dedicated to living godly lives and twenty percent to how we conduct worship services. I believe the truer numbers are in the 90/10 or 95/5 range, but even 80/20 numbers are significant.

And, in the New Testament readings, it is difficult to tell if the passage is talking about things we are supposed to be doing during "worship service" or outside "worship service." It just seems to be all blended together—which would make sense if our spiritual act of worship is offering our bodies as living sacrifices.

If I look at it closely, there is not much separation in the New Testament dialogue between "worship service" and "daily lives." It seems more in line with the text to say that our entire life is a worship service, part of which includes that one hour on Sunday, which leaves a whole lot of hours that it covers outside that brief time.

A Message to Adult Bible Class Teachers

Many years ago, I told the education minister of a fairly large congregation, where I worshiped, that if an adult class teaching opportunity came up I would like to be considered to fill it. I had never taught an adult Bible class, but knew that, if I had to teach, it would force me to study. In other words, because of my lack of self discipline, I wanted a crutch.

About two weeks later, he called me and said that, beginning the next quarter, he was starting another class and wanted me to teach it. I was in business.

I felt so sorry for my class members for the first few months. I was such a lousy teacher. I wanted it to be a discussion class but it just was not working. I was boring myself to death and had a hard time generating discussion.

I could not believe the class members would keep coming back, but they did and I appreciated them for it. I knew that to become good, I had to go through this phase of being bad—a crawl before you walk, type thing.

As a personal crutch, however, this was working. I was so terrified that someone would ask me to back up, with scripture, what I was saying, that I did not say anything unless I had a specific reason for saying it. To make sure I could back up every single statement, I was studying many hours each week, and that was good.

Because of this deep study, I was discovering things I had never known before. I would get so excited about these discoveries that I couldn't wait to come to class to share them.

But when I would try to present to the class, I just was not capturing the essence of what I was trying to get across. There was so much information and so little time.

That is when I first realized that, really good teaching requires a two stage preparation. One must study to learn, and then, must prepare a method to most effectively deliver the most important information in the most digestible way.

Until that point in time, I had only been doing stage one, studying to learn. I had not been preparing the information for good delivery. This new understanding was a breakthrough in my life.

That is also when it dawned on me what was wrong with most Bible classes I had experienced. Most average Bible Class Teachers never really do the study to learn part—stage one. Their idea of studying and/or preparing was to find the verses that proved what they already believed and to then organize them into some kind of presentable format. In other words, they only did stage two.

If you only do stage two, you are stagnant because you are not learning anything new but you are only spending your time reviewing the propaganda.

That is why these classes are so boring. Everyone knows what questions are going to be asked and, everyone knows what the answers are supposed to be. As long as no one rocks the boat, the class is deemed acceptable.

When I had this breakthrough in understanding, my classes started to be more productive. I now had new information to present each week, as well as a plan to deliver it.

The discussions were better because the standard questions and answers were challenged. Anyone who gave a standard answer had to justify it as to whether or not that had validity where the rubber meets the road.

I started hearing some of the sweetest responses I had ever heard, responses like, "You know, that never did make complete sense to me until now;" or "I have always wondered about that but was afraid to question it."

The Bible came alive and really did apply to our daily lives. There were real answers and they did not always line up with the ways we had been taught. It was awesome.

So now I say to you "Test everything. Hold on to the good." (1 Thes. 5:21) If you teach, first study to learn, then prepare to deliver. The joy you will experience will be off the charts.

One other "eye-opening" recommendation I would like to make: Occasionally read each epistle, in its entirety, in one sitting, as you would read a letter you may have received from a loved one. Things often look different when taken as a whole rather than as a dissected portion. It helps keep the bigger picture in mind.

Post Script

I suspect that you, as a reader, fit into one of two basic groups of people. The first group, by far the smallest, would be described as those who are very strict in their doctrinal beliefs. These people are very adamant about the way things are supposed to be. These people are so confident in what they believe and why they believe it, that it is almost impossible to reach them, even if what they believe is in error. That is why so few of them will read this book. They are just locked in to a certain way of thinking.

If you are one of these people, I hope that at the very least I have planted some seeds of doubt about what you have been teaching and believing for all these years. I hope that, when you now see certain scriptures that you've used to condemn others, you will at least give it a second thought and pull back a little. That is a step in the right direction.

I suspect that when you started reading this book you had absolute confidence that it "would not phase you one bit." Hopefully you were wrong. Hopefully you've been phased, at least a little.

The second group is made up of people "in the middle." You are dedicated Christians, or at least you would like to be, yet you've not been as adamant about what the Bible teaches as those in the first group. You've sensed that what you've been taught does not seem exactly right, but you've never been able to put your finger on just what was wrong.

You've respected these confident brothers and sisters for the most part (though not always). They've seemed so positive about what they believe. But you do not like how eager they have been to condemn others. Surely they must be right. But still . . ..

I suspect that you are now feeling liberated. You are feeling released from bondage and invigorated by the prospect of freedom in Christ. You are ready to dig in to the Word with eagerness to see what God has in store for you. You wish, with all your heart, that those from the first group would read the book, would change. But you are joyful regardless.

You, in this second group, especially, bring me great joy. You make me so happy. You will no longer need to be held hostage to legalistic regulations in worship ever again. Or will you?

One thing I have noticed about myself is that, even though I know that the regulations for worship have been done away with, it is difficult to completely purge them from my system. They have been so deeply ingrained into my being. They cling to me like barnacles on a boat. Bad habits die hard.

I have seen the same thing in others. We can all fully acknowledge the truth, that there are no regulations for worship, and then proceed to feel uncomfortable if anything is done during a service that might violate one of the old rules. It is just human nature that it makes us uncomfortable.

For what it is worth, I have a suggestion. Start off by just refusing to condemn others for doing things differently. One of our unfortunate traits has been that we have sometimes been so eager to condemn others. Do not be doing it any more. Or, if you have not been doing it, be bold enough to tell people you are not going to do it—that you think we have been wrong to do so.

According to the Bible, we are supposed to be known for our love. Unfortunately, we have more often been known (myself included) for our self-righteous and judgmental attitudes. You do not have to go far into the community to know the truth of that (if you can find someone bold enough to be honest about it).

For years I would not invite friends to come to church with me because I knew that if I ever got them in the door, one time, that they would never come back again. I wanted to wait until things got better before inviting them. I did not know if it ever would.

Thank God it is not that way for me now. I am in a very loving and gracious congregation, for which I thank God almost daily. What a blessing it is.

We do not focus on rule-keeping, though most of what we do looks amazingly similar to what we did when we were focused on rule-keeping. We focus on spiritual battery charging, caring and lifting up, comforting and supporting, and praising God with our songs and prayers of thanksgiving.

We do not have any score-keepers or referees who are making sure we stay in the boundaries. We just love, and praise, and laugh and sing. What a blessing it is.

And that is what I wish for you.

Thank you for taking the time to read this book. I hope it has blessed your life. Please share it and encourage others to read it. Use is as a resource for Bible study groups. Spread the word. Make a difference. I would love to hear from you. Please email me at

tal@dennisensor.com

Let me know what resonated with you. And let me know how you are doing. From the bottom of my heart I ask God's blessings on you and yours. Stay in touch.

Website: www.tal.dennisensor.com

1. Allen, C. Leonard, *Distant Voices: Discovering a Forgotten Past for a Changing Church*, (Abilene, TX: ACU Press, 1993)

2. Woodroof, Tim, *A Church That Flies: A New Call to Restoration in the Churches of Christ*, (Leafwood Publishing, 2000), 103

Taking Another Look at New Testament Christianity

can be **purchased online** from

Amazon.com

or

https://www.createspace.com/4762495

or

in bulk from Dennis Ensor at

www.tal.dennisensor.com

Taking Another Look is available in paperback and in the Kindle format.

If you would like to

- Subscribe to the TAL newsletter,
- Be added to the discount promo notification list,
- Read the TAL blog,
- Be notified of TAL updates
- Make comments or
- Be a part of the N.T. Christianity discussion

go to the following website:

www.tal.dennisensor.com

~~~~~

You can reach me by email at

tal@dennisensor.com

You can also reach me by **snail mail** at
Dennis Ensor
439 CR 220
Hamilton TX 76531

The **Good News From God** book can be downloaded (in eight languages), free of charge, at

www.goodnewsfromgodbook.wordpress.com

May God bless you as you study his Word!

Made in the USA
Lexington, KY
13 June 2015